UNIVERSITY STUDENTS
BEHAVING BADLY

UNIVERSITY STUDENTS BEHAVING BADLY

Deborah Lee

Trentham Books

Stoke on Trent, UK and Sterling, USA

Trentham Books Limited

Westview House	22883 Quicksilver Drive
734 London Road	Sterling
Oakhill	VA 20166-2012
Stoke on Trent	USA
Staffordshire	
England ST4 5NP	

First published 2006

British Library Cataloguing-in-Publication Data
A catalogue record for this book is available from the
British Library

ISBN-10: 1-85856-369-0
ISBN-13: 978-1-85856-369-5

Designed and typeset by Trentham Print Design Ltd, Chester
and printed in Great Britain by Bemrose Shafron (Printers) Ltd,
Chester.

Contents

For my mother, Pamela Lee

Acknowledgements

This research was supported by a Nuffield Small Grant (Ref: SGS/00671/G). I would like to thank Beth Claridge, Marie Parker-Jenkins, Elizabeth Stanko, Morwenna Griffiths, Pamela Abbott, Paul Weller and Louise Richards for their assistance with my grant application and everyone who subsequently publicised the project at UK higher education institutions. I am very grateful to my respondents for participating in the research. I would like to thank Beverley Lyons for secretarial assistance, Steve Farrar and Phil Baty at the *Times Higher Education Supplement* for their interest in the project, and Ellen Annandale and Joanna Liddle for help with references. Special thanks are extended to Gillian Klein, Val Walsh, Dawn Forman and Pamela Cotterill, who offered much appreciated advice and encouragement during the writing process; and Graham Fowler, who lived with the project from start to finish.

A version of Chapter Three appeared as: Lee, Deborah. Students and managers behaving badly: an exploratory analysis of the vulnerability of feminist academics in anti-feminist, market-driven UK higher education, *Women's Studies International Forum*, 28, 2-3, pp 195-208, Copyright (2005). It is reproduced here by kind permission of Elsevier.

Introduction

While I was conducting the research for this book a journalist contacted me, interested to know what sorts of 'unacceptable student conduct towards academics in UK higher education' my project was revealing. At the time I was not ready to share my data so the journalist spoke to several academics and decided that: 'mobile phones seem to top the lecturer's whinge list ... other inappropriate behaviour ... includes sleeping, eating and drinking during lectures ...' There were a couple 'necking' in one of my lectures recently' said one tutor indignantly' (Coxon, 2002). These are some of the ways academics experience 'unacceptable student conduct'.

University Students Behaving Badly, however, reveals student-perpetrated physical attacks, stalking, verbal abuse, sexual remarks delivered in person, by email and anonymous telephone call, complaints of poor teaching and supervision made via student feedback questionnaires or directly to university managers and the often appalling ways in which university managers respond to these incidents.

The research project

The main data source for this book is semi-structured qualitative interviews with academics who have encountered unacceptable student conduct; a questionnaire was also distributed to personnel professionals at UK universities (see Chapter Six).

Interviewees were self-selected and recruited via the letters page of the *Lecturer* (the National Association of Teachers in Further and Higher Education [NATFHE] members' newspaper), the diary section of the *Times Higher Education Supplement* (*THES*), the Association of University Teachers (AUT) email group for women academics and all-staff emails sent for me by individuals at a range of pre-

1992 and post-1992 universities. Though I tried to use the AUT email groups for Black and lesbian/gay academics this proved impossible to arrange. The appeals for respondents asked:

> Are you an academic who has encountered unacceptable student conduct? My research, which is funded by the Nuffield Foundation, seeks to explore what sorts of unacceptable student conduct academics encounter. Perhaps disrespect in the classroom or office, unfair course evaluations, malicious complaints, offensive emails, bullying, personal remarks, sexual innuendo, unwanted physical contact, sexual harassment, stalking? My main concern is to discover what you have experienced as unacceptable student conduct. I am interested in the experiences of all academic staff. The problems academics encounter with students are seriously under-researched in the UK. So, if you would like to be interviewed for this research, please contact me. I assure you that your experiences will be treated in the strictest confidence.

People who telephoned or emailed in response to these appeals expressed delight that I was conducting the study; they were all keen to tell me about their experiences. Prior to interviews taking place I provided everyone with a research information sheet and an informed consent form, which were consistent with the British Sociological Association (BSA) statement of ethical practice with reference to relationships with research participants (www.britsoc. co.uk). Everyone remained eager to participate after reviewing the research information sheet and informed consent form.

I interviewed twenty-two people, who were primarily reporting experiences which had occurred in the last five years. Ten were women and twelve men. Seven were from pre-1992 universities and fifteen from post-1992 universities. Their ages ranged from 25 to 65. Their job titles ran from Graduate Teaching Assistant to Principal Lecturer and they were employed in a wide range of academic disciplines all of which have been changed along with other identifying details. They were all white; no one identified as lesbian, gay, bisexual or transgender; only two male respondents said they had disabilities, one an unseen disability and one a disability due to a recent accident. No one mentioned class or religion as an issue.

At the time of the interviews I was a 30 year-old Lecturer in Sociology at a post-1992 university. I am white, non-disabled, heterosexual, partnered and childfree. My interest in this area of research developed from my previous studies of sexual harassment and bullying (Lee, 1998, 2000a, 2000b, 2001 and 2002a) and my experiences of academic employment.

The structure of the book

This book draws primarily upon feminist sociology, and incorporates analyses from education, staff development, psychology, criminology, healthcare and human resource management.

In Chapter One I review selected research conducted in Europe, North America and Australia which explores sexual harassment, bullying and violence at work: discourses which have been chosen as a consequence of the types of experiences respondents reported and the self-reported characteristics of these respondents. My analysis recognises that unacceptable workplace conduct is increasingly understood not just as a superior attacking a subordinate in an organisational hierarchy but in terms of doctors and nurses being propositioned by their patients and schoolchildren bullying their teachers. There is an element of blaming victims when analyses of sexual harassment, bullying and violence shift beyond mistreatment by superiors and peers in organisational hierarchies. Consequently, as analysis of unacceptable student conduct in UK higher education develops, blaming victims should be avoided.

Chapters Two to Five draw upon empirical material. I analyse selected interviews in detail, rather than provide a broad overview. My contention is that a deep exploration of accounts provided by interviewees is required at this early point in understanding unacceptable student conduct and subsequent managerial intervention in higher education.

At the beginning of Chapter Two, I note that reasons why such experiences have not yet been properly recognised in academia are the currency of the common-sense views that only inexperienced academics encounter problems with students and that these are the result of inexperience on the part of the academic. I use interviews with two women graduate teaching assistants and two women early career academics to start to replace victim-blaming with a more sophisticated consideration of how academic status can make teachers vulnerable both to student misconduct and to inappropriate management intervention.

Chapter Three reveals that it is not just new and relatively new academics who experience problems with students and managers. I focus upon a richly detailed interview to show how feminist identification can make an academic vulnerable. I suggest that the standard reading of staff-student problems as teacher inadequacy may be subverted by deploying the interpretation 'contrapower sexual harassment'. This recognises that: 'women in positions of authority within a university or a business can be subjected to harassment by men who occupy formally less powerful positions within those institutions' (Benson, 1984:518).

In Chapter Four, I shift beyond new and relatively new women academics and feminist-identified academic women to explore how any women academics may be vulnerable to the problems revealed in this book. I draw upon interviews with two women academics and demonstrate how sexism can be the premise for inappropriate managerial interventions. This draws together Chapters Two, Three and Four, stressing that women's experiences of unacceptable student conduct and subsequent managerial intervention need to be located in the current context of pervasive sexism in the academy.

Chapter Five demonstrates that men, too, can be victims. I focus upon five men who have encountered similar experiences to the women in Chapters Two, Three and Four. A recognition of men's experiences could prompt a rethinking of sexist responses to academic women's experiences, yet the way in which men can be feminised by oppression is shown to undermine that contention. In this chapter, I evaluate the interpretation 'workplace bullying', but conclude that 'violence in higher education' is currently the most appropriate description to use to propose a campaign in the academy.

Chapter Six outlines the proposed campaign. It would involve promoting self-help activities, institutional audits, revisions to policies and procedures, risk assessments, personal safety measures, professional development and networking. Appropriate managerial intervention is needed for these interventions to be successful and the current character of UK higher education must undergo significant cultural change if the problem of unacceptable student conduct is to be tackled.

My end note brings together the threads of the previous chapters and proposes how this field of research might develop. This book is just a starting point in analysing unacceptable student conduct in higher education. My position parallels Letherby (2002: 3.9): I do not seek to offer the 'absolute truth' of university students behaving badly but to be 'widening the debate surrounding [this] issue'. The intention is to put an end to the question I have been asked constantly whilst conducting this research: 'does that [unacceptable student conduct towards academics] really happen then?'

1

A brief history of sexual harassment, bullying and violence at work

This chapter explores the sexual harassment, bullying and violence at work debates from a feminist sociological perspective. A wide range of studies have explored these topics so my review is selective rather than exhaustive. I draw from studies which have been conducted internationally and focus particularly upon compulsory education and healthcare, as these settings provide reference points for my analysis. Studies exploring student mistreatment of academics are not included, as so few analyses currently exist. The sexual harassment, bullying and violence at work debates often reveal an ambivalence towards mistreatment of staff by non-staff. This ambivalence is important to note at the outset of this book which aims to provide sustained analysis of unacceptable student conduct towards academics in UK higher education.

Sexual harassment

Women have always encountered unwanted male sexual conduct in the workplace, yet the deployment of a specific concept to interpret such experiences was not developed until the 1970s. Farley (1978) reports that a consciousness-raising session for women took place at Cornell University in the US, at which each of the participants revealed that they had: 'quit or been fired from a job at least once because [they] had been made too uncomfortable by the behaviour of men' (pxi). The interpretation 'sexual harassment' was chosen to describe the problem.

A questionnaire was then distributed to ascertain the prevalence of sexual harassment, defined as: 'any repeated and unwanted sexual comments, looks, suggestions or physical contact that you find objectionable or offensive and cause you discomfort on your job' (Farley, 1978:20). All manifestations of unwanted male sexual conduct, rather than just demands for sex, were therefore legitimate causes of complaint for, as Farley notes (p15), they all contribute 'to the ultimate goal of keeping women subordinate at work'. The questionnaire received 155 responses from self-selected women respondents, 70 per cent of whom said that they had encountered sexual harassment.

Farley recognised that few women complained when faced with sexual harassment because: 'society trains women to be 'nice''. She also recognised that leaving a job instead of objecting to sexual harassment promised 'the best chance of obtaining future work' (p23). Thus, she did not pathologise women for not objecting to a problem for which society blames them anyway; instead she wanted to draw attention to the unacceptability of unwanted male sexual conduct.

The concept of 'sexual harassment' migrated from the US to other countries, including the UK, in the 1980s (Wise and Stanley, 1987). In the UK, a survey conducted for the Alfred Marks Bureau in 1982 showed that 60 per cent of women respondents had encountered unwanted male sexual conduct at work (Hadjifotiou, 1983). British writers, such as Hadjifotiou, concurred with Farley that sexual harassment did not just involve demands for sex. The difficulty for women of seeking redress when sexual harassment had occurred was also recognised. Hadjifotiou (1983:23) comments that 'managements are reluctant to discipline or dismiss supervisors or male workers. Their skills are seen as more valuable'. Like Farley, Hadjifotiou did not blame women for their experiences. Writing from a trade union perspective, she simply noted that in the circumstances where 'the most common reaction to a complaint of sexual harassment is that a woman 'asked for it'', 'your credibility when making a complaint may increase if you cannot easily be accused of provocation or of misleading the harasser' (p60).

It is clear that early researchers did not hold women responsible for sexual harassment. Research has subsequently noted that women who are young and unmarried are the most likely victims of sexual harassment, but 'older individuals, married people, and men have not been immune' (Stockdale, 1996:7). The emphasis of the debate has therefore not been upon seeking to uncover the perceived shortcomings of the sexually harassed because anyone can encounter the problem. Instead, drawing from a clearly feminist perspective, the focus has been and remains upon: 'ways in which harassment stands as a manifestation of a wider system of asymmetrical power relations between men and women in society' (Thomas, 1997:134).

This recognition of gendered power relations has affected the presentation of harassers as well as victims. Most research has stressed that 'the harasser's motivation and intentions should be irrelevant when it comes to deciding whether or not a given incident constitutes harassment' (Thomas, 1997:131): whether or not sexual harassment has occurred is seen to be in the 'eye of the beholder' (Wise and Stanley, 1987:158). This is not to say that analyses of why men harass have not been produced or are not still being produced. There are instances of this line of enquiry from the 1980s to the present day (e.g. Dziech and Weiner, 1984; Fitzgerald and Weitzman, 1990; Kosson et al, 1997; O'Leary-Kelly et al, 2000; Rapaport and Burkhart, 1984; Zalk, 1990; Lucero et al, 2003). However, while writers drawing primarily upon psychological approaches have developed typologies of sexual harassers, the proposition that: 'there are the minority of harassers and the majority [of men] who are OK' (Wise and Stanley, 1987:7) is not acceptable to most feminist researchers, who are concerned with the power dynamics which are in play when women encounter sexual harassment.

Thomas (1997) has made an important contribution to the analysis of sexual harassers by taking a feminist psycho-social approach to the topic. She explores men's views of sexual harassment and demonstrates that indulging in sexual harassment is not individual pathology but: 'recognisably 'normal' behaviour, in so far as most men at some point in their lives are likely to practise it in some form or other' (p148). Thomas draws attention to the pressure upon men to engage in misogyny and says that 'by acknowledging the coercive and corrosive aspects of patriarchal power that they themselves experience, men may at last be in a position to understand that rejecting the patriarchal imperative could in fact be liberating for all' (p150). This moves analysis of sexual harassers beyond ignoring or pathologising them and offers ways forward from a position in which men will seemingly always be sexual harassers. Thomas's contribution demonstrates one way in which there has been a fruitful rethinking of the sexual harassment debate (Brant and Too, 1994a).

The process of rethinking sexual harassment has also involved recognition that sexual harassment is not just conventionally 'sexual' conduct encountered in the workplace by women. Wise and Stanley (1987:4) have attempted to extend the sexual harassment discourse by defining the problem as 'unwanted and intrusive male behaviour ... forced on women'. They give the example of a woman whose father switches off a television programme she is watching so that she can listen to him instead. Alternatively, in previous research (Lee, 2001), I have explored whether terms such as 'sexism' may be more useful to women in drawing attention to conduct which they find offensive (see also Epstein, 1997). The sexual harassment experiences of school girls (e.g. Jones, 1985; Halson, 1991; Herbert, 1989) have been explored, as have women's experiences of sexual harassment at university (e.g. Hall and Sandler, 1984; Dzeich and Weiner, 1984; Lee, 1998; Wilson, 2000; Eyre, 2001). In previous work (Lee, 2000b), I explored the sexual harassment of heterosexual men by heterosexual men and women. Epstein (1997) has analysed the sexual harassment experiences of men who are gay or perceived to be gay and Kitzinger (1994) has explored the sexual harassment of lesbian women. Equally, while Black women's experiences of sexual harassment were noted in early research (e.g. Farley, 1978), more recently there have been analyses which develop understanding of race and sexual harassment (see Murrell, 1996). In these studies, the initial sympathy for sexual harassment victims exemplified by early writers such as Farley and Hadjifotiou has remained, even when the focus of enquiry has shifted beyond the traditional conceptualisation of sexual harassment as a white, heterosexual woman encountering unwelcome male sexual conduct at work.

What has been called the 'sexual harassment industry' (Patai, 1998) has been questioned by researchers who may be viewed as approaching the topic from an anti-feminist perspective. Patai feels that *quid pro quo* sexual harassment is 'the true sexual shakedown' – everything else she perceives as attempts by the 'sexual harassment industry' to oversee 'virtually the entire social scene' (p103). This argument is incorrect: sexual harassment research is not a closed field which only accepts one way of viewing the world. Lerum (2004) explores sexuality and sexual harassment in service work. She claims that while sexualised banter between co-workers can 'facilitate sexual harassment, cultural isolation and the social control and exploitation of workers', there are circumstances in which it can: 'assist a process of heightened morale and worker camaraderie' (p758).

Roiphe (1994:101-2), well-known as an anti-feminist contributor to the sexual harassment debate, seems to object to the idea that women are able to define any conduct as sexual harassment, maintaining that women: 'should be learning to deal with individuals with strength and confidence ... without crying into our pillows or screaming for help or counselling...'. Samuels (2003), writing from a feminist legal perspective, disagrees: she feels that complaint is empowering, rather than an indication of victimisation. Brewis and Linstead (2000), meanwhile, are critical of the sexual harassment discourse: they say that they do not want to 'persuade women of their essential vulnerability' (Brewis and Linstead, 2000:91), yet even they find Roiphe's approach unconvincing:

> What Roiphe implies ... is that women ought to be able to con-
> sciously control not only their own behaviour but that of others –
> that is to say, men's – as well ... Therefore, while [Roiphe's ap-
> proach] does go some way towards questioning the certainties of
> harassment discourse, it immediately replaces these certainties
> with its own – that women must be accountable for their own be-
> haviour *and* the behaviour of others towards them. (Brewis and
> Linstead, 2000:91, italics in original)

So although victim-blaming is not a feature of most research into sexual harassment, there is, surprisingly, one area where sympathy for the victim is not always forthcoming from researchers, even those whose stance is not anti-feminist. That is when the perpetrator is not a superior or peer in an organisational hierarchy and the victim is a woman professional employee. This contrasts with the usually sympathetic portrayal by researchers of instances where women encounter sexual harassment from customers whilst employed in service jobs (Adkins, 1995) and when women managers encounter sexual harassment from male subordinates (Cockburn, 1991).

Professional women's experiences of sexual harassment by non-employees is not newly-identified. It was first recognised in the 1980s, when Hadjifotiou (1983) said that women encounter sexual harassment in what she termed the 'feminine professions' such as nursing and teaching. She observed that nurses are portrayed as there 'to rebuild the self-confidence of male patients by reinforcing their masculinity through reference to their obvious, if temporarily impaired, sexual prowess and attraction' (p44), so it is not surprising that they are sexually harassed by them. And she noted that teachers are vulnerable to sexual harassment from pupils of all ages but particularly from adolescent boys.

Early research in this area shows how the problem of sexual harassment by non-employees can be theorised to the disadvantage of victims. Whitbread (1989) offers an analysis of female teachers and pupils taking action against sexual harassment by school boys. She points out that new women members of staff and women students on teaching practice were the principal targets of sexual harassment and says that: 'this is not surprising ... women in low status positions are more likely to be treated as mere objects for male titillation than women with more authority in the work situation' (p91). This is an example of sexual harassment being seen simplistically and unhelpfully as a consequence of women's professional inexperience.

Inappropriate client sexual conduct, patients who act provokingly and contrapower sexual harassment in healthcare

Schneider *et al*'s (1999) article exploring inappropriate client sexual behaviour (ICSB) in allied healthcare in Australia provides a more current analysis of unwelcome sexual conduct towards women professionals by people who are not the women's superiors or peers in organisational hierarchies. Schneider *et al* say that 'whereas once it may have been both expected and accepted that health professionals have to deal with 'difficult' clients, ICSB is now open to being interpreted and labelled as sexual harassment'. The way this point is expressed is important: ICSB is now '*open to* being interpreted and labelled as sexual harassment' (p177, italics added). This implies exactly what Schneider *et al* go on to say; the view that health professionals should be able to deal with 'difficult' clients remains: 'there is a recognition in the nursing literature that when sexual harassment is perpetrated by a patient or client towards a health professional, the primary responsibility for stopping it lies with the health professional' (p179).

This tension between conceptualising health professionals as sexually harassed or responsible for dealing with ICSB is clear from Schneider *et al*'s own research, which is the first Australian study of ICSB in occupational therapy. Questionnaires were posted to 202 occupational therapists; 144 questionnaires were returned, a response rate of 76.2 per cent; 97.9 per cent of these respondents were female. Questionnaires revealed that 72.9 per cent of the respondents had experienced ICSB – 98.2 per cent of it perpetrated by male clients towards female therapists. Most respondents had encountered sexual remarks, jokes, touching or requests for dates.

Schneider *et al* (1999:189) draw upon Gutek and Morasch (1982) to say that male clients may see women occupational therapists as women and thus may '[treat] the therapist as they would a woman generally, that is, as a potential personal relationship or sexual partner'. This is consistent with a conceptualisation of the woman occupational therapist as sexually harassed. In such circumstances it would be inappropriate to propose that the sexually harassed woman should learn how to deal with sexual harassment: instead, the male perpetrator would be expected to take responsibility for the sexual harassment. Yet, in healthcare, the situation is not so straightforward. Respondents to Schneider *et al*'s survey noted that ICSB 'often related to a client's cognitive (42 per cent), or psychosocial (33.9 per cent) performance component deficit, or a combination of both (21.4 per cent)' (p186). These factors in clients indicate that ICSB may always be present in occupational therapy.

Their survey reveals that whilst occupational therapists think that new recruits should be prepared for ICSB, they do not view ICSB as unproblematic. A respondent remarked that healthcare professionals need: 'information about what constitutes harassment, therapists' rights, what measures to take in continuing to treat the client/family, for example, another staff member present?' (p191). Nevertheless, Schneider *et al*'s research demonstrates that occupational therapists often do not conceptualise ICSB as sexual harassment. Schneider *et al* remark that this may be because 'most occupational therapists seem to have attributed the cause of ICSB as external to the client, to have perceived such behaviours as unintentional, or non-hostile, and unlikely to recur' (p190). They refer to a lack of acceptance that ICSB occurs in occupational therapy and say that this has led to contrapower sexual harassment not being recognised. Yet is it necessary for occupational therapists to characterise ICSB as contrapower sexual harassment? The rethinking sexual harassment debate (Epstein, 1997; Lee, 2001) proposes that women cannot be forced to deploy the concept of sexual harassment; instead a range of ways in which women can conceptualise unwanted conduct should be validated. Given that occupational therapists are seemingly more comfortable referring to ICSB than sexual harassment, ICSB is perhaps the interpretation required for these healthcare professionals in order to call for the 'institutional policies for the management of the incidents [of ICSB]' that Schneider *et al* (1999:179) anticipate will be developed following their research.

Scandinavian health researchers Hellzen *et al* (2004) explore the meaning of caring as described by women nurses caring for a male patient 'who acts provokingly'. Their article demonstrates the importance of effective management, and the consequences for pro-

7

fessionals when this is lacking. The women nurses they interviewed cared for a male patient with learning difficulties who sexually harassed fellow patients and nurses. While it should not be presumed that people with disabilities are asexual (Browne and Russell, 2005), what these nurses experienced is highly problematic. For instance, one nurse said: 'to be seen as a sexual attribute, a whore or a pussy, every day, breaks me down ... I can't stand it' (Hellzen *et al*, 2004:7). Nurses reported that:

> When we ask our chiefs for help they don't understand. The only thing we hear from them is: he's better now than before and *if you can't manage him*, phone a taxi and send him to the big supermarket outside the city. There he can calm himself down by drinking coffee and being with people. (Hellzen *et al*, 2004:8 italics added)

This advice was humiliating for the nurses, who said they 'needed a supervisor who understands and the only way to understand is to have personal experience of being hit, spat at and exposed to sexual harassment ... and where can we find someone like that?' (p8).

The way in which Hellzen *et al* conducted their research highlights the fact that researchers, and not just victims and their managers, can engage in victim-blaming. The research involved asking nurses their views of the patient, an outline of an ordinary day at the institution and for examples of 'difficult caring situations that *you resolved well or badly*' (p4, italics added). The premise of the study seems to be that nurses have to take responsibility for what happens in the institution. They explain however that: 'nobody should be allowed to act in the way the patient did nor should anybody be allowed to receive such humiliations from another person as they had done', but unfortunately their unease with sexual harassment of professional women by non-employees has already been implied.

Their research focuses upon a patient who is considered not to be able to behave any differently, so what happens may be distinct from how 'acting provokingly' might be viewed elsewhere. Thus, in this instance, the recommendation that 'a way to help the nurses to stand humiliations could probably be through debriefing and supervision' (Hellzen *et al*, 2004:9) may be appropriate. Moving beyond this approach, the sexual well-being of people with disabilities is rarely considered (Browne and Russell, 2005), and it may be that exploring ways to achieve this would be more helpful than seeking to blame nurses who are distressed by a patient who acts provokingly. As it stands, Hellzen *et al*'s research shows that an approach to unacceptable conduct which may be suitable for a particular healthcare setting should not be simplistically replicated in other areas.

There is contrapower sexual harassment research in healthcare which offers a largely sympathetic understanding of healthcare professionals who are sexually harassed by patients. Schneider and Phillips (1997) provide a qualitative study of sexual harassment of female doctors by patients in Canada. They observe that when a woman physician is sexually harassed by a patient, she 'may interpret this to mean that she has not been able to maintain her professional stance' (p675), but they make it clear that they do not agree with this interpretation.

They also reveal that: 'some of the reported incidents would not be considered to be sexual harassment as defined in most existing research. They are nonetheless incidents which were somewhat disturbing to physicians, who were prompted to write about the incidents in the context of a study of sexual harassment' (p672). Thus what constitutes sexual harassment needs to be constantly reviewed, particularly when the victims are encountering sexual harassment which is not perpetrated by a superior or a peer in an organisational hierarchy.

Nevertheless, physicians felt constrained when they encountered sexual harassment from a patient because they feared that the patient might make a complaint against them. This is highly relevant to healthcare professionals. Annandale's (1996) analysis of risk culture in nursing in the UK illustrates this. She says that few of her respondents had actually been the subject of a complaint from a patient but that: 'it is what people take to be real that has real consequences' (Annandale, 1996:425 quoting Dingwall, 1994).

Schneider and Phillips (1997) conclude that: 'female family physicians, and medical students, could benefit from professional training in dealing with harassment' (p676). This is an unfortunate end point, as it takes sexual harassment as a given. What we should consider instead is how patients can be encouraged to behave less inappropriately towards physicians.

So far, we have explored research which focuses upon the experiences of healthcare professionals. Perhaps healthcare professionals are simply expected to take responsibility for the conduct of their patients because they are seen as too unwell to know what they are doing? So is victim-blaming present when the perpetrators of unacceptable conduct are not unwell?

The sexualisation and sexual harassment of school teachers by pupils

Education researchers from Finland, Lahelma *et al* (2000), draw upon ethnographic interviews and observations at two secondary schools and letters and telephone calls received in response to contributions to a trade union journal to explore the 'sexualisation' and 'sexual harassment' of female and male teachers by students. They say that: 'when teachers have reacted with strong emotions of anxiety, shame or embarrassment to students' verbal, physical or written acts of sexualisation [sexualisation is being defined as: 'all kinds of comments in which teachers are addressed as sexual persons'], the term sexual harassment can be used' (p465).

Teachers may not always be willing to identify themselves as being affected by the conduct of pupils: consequently, they would not apply the term 'sexual harassment' to their experiences. Thus, the way in which Lahelma *et al* characterise 'sexualisation' and 'sexual harassment' is problematic and may contribute to the persistence of professionals choosing not to interpret contrapower sexual harassment as such.

Their article nevertheless highlights how power relations are implicated in the sexualisation and sexual harassment of women and men teachers. They explain that: 'the female teacher is in a position of power *vis-à-vis* her students but male students can challenge her power by sexualising her and thus naming her gender' (Lahelma *et al*, 2000:468). Men teachers, meanwhile 'may feel objectified, embarrassed and confused, but by evoking masculinity they can retrieve their superior position in power relations'. For instance, one male respondent referred to a female pupil sending him rather innocent sexual messages. He asked her to stay behind and 'explained to her that it was not a good idea for a good-looking girl to be playing with fire'.

Teachers who said that they had been harmed by their experiences of sexualisation and sexual harassment reported that what had happened was:

> ... difficult to forget, and the incidents have continued to trouble them even years after. ... [They] were sometimes astonished and annoyed when they realised how deeply they felt hurt by an apparently small incident. They felt that, as professional teachers, they should be able to deal with these kinds of situations, and felt embarrassed when they recognised their own lack of skills. (Lahelma *et al*, 2000:470)

That they recognised their 'own lack of skills' implies that the teachers should have possessed the skills to respond to and recover easily from sexual harassment. Saying that the teachers: 'felt embarrassed by what they perceived as their lack of skills' would have been more appropriate, unless Lahelma *et al* really wish to propose that teachers should feel embarrassed by their reactions and responses to sexual harassment.

Disappointingly, as the authors develop their exploration of how teachers have responded to sexualisation and sexual harassment, that interpretation starts to seem plausible. They explain that teachers can choose to 'side-step' sexualisation, because they cannot think of a response, they fear provoking the student, they feel that responding would be giving the student the attention they are looking for or because they are upset or frightened. Alternatively, teachers might join in with sexualisation. However, the authors seem clear that they only condone an immediate response to sexualisation and sexual harassment because:

> Teachers ... have a responsibility for the atmosphere in schools: are young students allowed to address their teachers or peers in sexualising or harassing ways, or is this kind of behaviour strictly forbidden? This may remain unclear in situations when teachers join in the joking. (Lahelma *et al*, 2000:475)

While this statement explicitly refers to teachers who join in with sexualisation, which is inappropriate, the subtext is that responses of confusion or fear when confronted with sexual harassment or sexualisation are disallowed.

Lahelma *et al* say that discussion of sexualisation and sexual harassment is required in schools because if this does not happen then 'the problem can easily become a problem of one specific person: a teacher who is unable to deal with the situation or a student who harasses' (p477). This is important as it introduces the idea that it is not simply the professional who needs to be trained to deal with the issue (see Schneider and Phillips, 1997), but the students as well. They conclude:

> If teachers cannot find ways to confront sexualisation and sexual harassment that is directed to themselves, it is difficult for them to work towards a school community in which sex-based harassment that is directed at girls, and sometimes at boys, does not occur. This is a challenge that teacher education should face. (p476)

This assumes that the starting point for dealing with sex-based harassment is that this is taking place: sex-based harassment is a given. It is difficult to know what to do about it and the messages are rather mixed: recognition of a serious problem in schools which affects teachers deeply, but a subtext that teachers should deal with the problem, for the benefit of their pupils. Of course pupils matter, but teachers matter too.

In contrast, Robinson (2000) offers an excellent exploration of the sexual harassment of women teachers by school boys in secondary schools in Australia. Using a sociological perspective, Robinson argues that boys in her study did not fear the repercussions of engaging in sexual harassment because male staff and students understood sexual harassment as simply an outcome of the ineffective discipline strategies of women teachers. One woman teacher remarked that: 'If your class mucks up and you are female ... it is seen as a result of you being female. When a male's class mucks up it is seen to be the result of a different reason, a problem at home, or a problem with the student or something' (p83). Much as we saw in healthcare, Robinson notes 'a stereotype operating in schools that hides the extent and nature of the sexual harassment of female teachers by boys': perpetrators were constructed as 'other' (for example, lower-ability boys were viewed as 'not capable of controlling their sexual behaviour' [p86]), and that this means that 'gender and power inequalities entrenched in patriarchal societal structures, practices and relationships' (p88) do not have to be considered. She maintains that how sexual harassment operates in schools has to be understood in order to make interventions into the problem. This is a useful way to proceed.

Workplace bullying

'Workplace bullying' was first identified in Scandinavia in the 1980s, where it was referred to as 'mobbing' (Leymann, 1990). While 'there is no definitive list of bullying behaviours' (Rayner *et al*, 2002:9), workplace bullying can be interpreted as encompassing incidents such as:

> Setting objectives with impossible deadlines; removing areas of responsibility and giving people menial or trivial tasks to do instead; taking credit for other people's ideas; ignoring or excluding an individual by talking only to a third party to isolate another; withholding information; spreading malicious rumours; constantly undervaluing effort; persistent criticism. (Manufacturing, Science and Finance trade union [now Amicus], 1994)

The word 'persistent' in this definition is salient. For persistence has been a central feature of much workplace bullying research: as

Rayner *et al* (2002:9) observe, the experiences a victim encounters 'may seem innocuous, but put together they add up to a scenario which is destabilising and threatening to the person who receives them'.

The concept of workplace bullying migrated to the UK in the early 1990s (Adams, 1992). At that time, bullying was understood primarily as a problem afflicting children at school, so there was initial surprise that conduct associated with playgrounds could be happening to adults in workplaces. For instance, Drysdale, a radio producer, explains that she was at first unconvinced when she heard taped examples of workplace bullying provided by Andrea Adams for a proposed Radio 4 programme. She recalls that:

> Ten minutes into the first tape I was doodling on the pad in front of me beginning to feel irritated. Anne, a woman bank employee, recounted how her manager had ridiculed her in front of the others for her vegetarian eating habits. Her response at once suggested that Anne must be over-sensitive. Did she really have to resort to eating her lunch in the ladies' loo to escape his taunts? (Drysdale in Adams, 1992:4)

Drysdale soon was convinced, however. As Anne proceeded to explain how this man treated her co-workers, 'a picture of the manager in question slowly emerged: an autocrat capable of extreme unpleasantness who was mercilessly aggressive and frequently out of control' (p4).

The assumption that bullying could not really be a problem for adults in workplaces was quickly disrupted by quantitative research projects. One of the earliest studies was conducted by Rayner (1997). She surveyed 1,137 part-time students and found that 53 per cent had encountered workplace bullying. The latest large-scale study involved 5,300 employees from over 70 organisations in the public, private and voluntary sectors (Hoel and Cooper, 2000). As Rayner *et al* (2002:25) explain, this survey data indicates that: 'close to 2.5 million people can be considered as labelling themselves as having been bullied during the last six months'.

Yet despite recognition of the scale of such bullying, Drysdale's initial view that workplace bullying victims can be interpreted as 'over-sensitive' persists in the mainstream debate. This focus upon 'individual' characteristics is in contrast to the focus upon 'group' characteristics in the sexual harassment debate (Simpson and Cohen, 2004:165) and reflects the salience of psychological approaches to current workplace bullying research. Einarsen (1999:21) provides an overview of personality traits which can be said to be associated with workplace bullying victims: they can be perceived as 'over-achievers' who have 'unrealistic' views of themselves (who are, therefore, 'annoying' to their superiors and peers), 'anxious', 'naïve' or 'neurotic' people with 'low self-esteem'. Clearly, not all researchers choose to highlight the perceived personality defects of victims. Field (1996), for example, who has encountered workplace bullying, identifies instead a very positive set of victim attributes. Equally, it would be a misrepresentation to say that workplace bullying research has fixated upon uncovering the personalities of victims. Nevertheless, unease with workplace bullying victims is a discernible aspect of the main-stream workplace bullying debate, which is not paralleled in sexual harassment research. It is surprising that this should be so, given that the workplace bullying debate, like the sexual harassment debate, intends to promote dignity and respect for workers.

Workplace bullying research has explored perpetrators as well as victims, indeed Zapf (1999) feels that British research has focused upon perpetrators more than victims (e.g. Crawford in Adams, 1992). In this research, while the actions of bullies are not justified, these individuals seem to receive a reasonably sympathetic por-trayal. This is because bullies are often understood to have suffered in childhood. Summing up the topics of victims and perpetrators, Zapf's (1999:77) point that 'there is a difference between finding a cause and assigning guilt or responsibility' is useful. Workplace bullying research has not so far always managed to avoid the assign-ment of guilt.

However, the workplace bullying debate, like the sexual harassment debate, is developing. Rayner (1999) sets out to explore whether or not it is possible to profile typical victims and perpetrators of work-place bullying. She concludes that there is not yet enough data on these subjects and, more importantly, says that: 'it is possible that to examine the problem purely as an interpersonal issue may be mis-guided as other factors (for example the environment) may mitigate or mediate the process' (p34). In subsequent work, Rayner *et al* (2002:107) agree that 'factors other than personality ... are important in deciding who gets bullied' and state that it has not yet been possible to identify a bully personality: indeed, no-one can claim that they have never bullied. This draws us back to Thomas's (1997) discussion of sexual harassers. Thomas says that seeking typologies: 'has the apparent advantage of offering society the possibility of pathologising and blaming a few individuals for their actions, while maintaining the comfortable illusion that the rest of society is blameless' (p133). Rayner *et al*'s observations indicate that we may now see a shift away from a focus upon individuals in workplace bullying research.

So far, workplace bullying has been explored without reference to the personal identities of the victims and perpetrators, for instance their sex and race. This has been consistent with the way workplace bullying research in contrast to sexual harassment research has developed: early contributions in this field (Adams, 1992; Field, 1996) insisted that workplace bullying was entirely a consequence of organisational power. Thus, Adams clearly differentiated bullying from sexual harassment.

When aspects of identities were finally explored in workplace bullying research, this was done in a way consistent with the quantitative research approach which has characterised many studies of workplace bullying: researchers explored how many women and men had been affected by the problem. For instance, in the Hoel and Cooper (2000) study, the data was analysed to see if men or women encountered more bullying, but: 'no statistically significant differences were found' (Rayner *et al*, 2002:28). This can be seen to make contributions to knowledge but does not offer a full understanding of the relevance of identities to workplace bullying.

However, Zapf (1999:72) has raised the question of whether people with disabilities are at a higher risk of being bullied in an organisation and says that if so, 'then this is a problem of the social group, which is not able to deal with people who are different. That is, the 'true cause' in such cases may lie in the social group and not in the victim'. This is an important point, echoed by Salin (2003:1219), who says that 'power differences associated with traditional gender roles and minority status may ... affect bullying behaviour, as it can be assumed that women and minorities are perceived to have less power and status'. This suggests the development of a more considered way to understand the relevance of identities to workplace bullying in contrast to the psychologising approach, focusing upon 'the motivations and feelings of the individual harasser' (Thomas, 1997:134). There is now a move to consider 'the ways in which [bullying] stands as a manifestation of a wider system of asymmetrical power relations between men and women in society' (Thomas, 1997:134). This is consistent with how Rayner *et al* (2002) propose that workplace bullying research should develop. They say that interviews and case studies, not just surveys, should be used as: 'such methodologies can gather information of a richer kind' (Rayner *et al*, 2002:186).

Detailed analyses which have been conducted to explore the dynamics of gender and race in women's and men's experiences of workplace bullying will follow. Bray (2001) has offered a gender analysis of the experiences of nurses in Canada, I have explored the gender dynamics of bullying in the UK Civil Service (Lee, 2002a), and Simpson and Cohen (2004) have looked at the gender dynamics of bullying in UK higher education. The research by Bray and Simpson and Cohen explores employment settings which are directly relevant to this book.

Simpson and Cohen's research involved distributing a questionnaire at one university (378 responses were received from a possible 1,900 people) and conducting a small number of interviews with self-selected informants. Two-thirds of the questionnaire responses were from women: 28.5 per cent of women and 19.8 per cent of men had been bullied; 67.5 per cent of women had witnessed bullying in comparison with 29.4 per cent of men. Simpson and Cohen report that more women than men had their decisions overruled. They relate this to men's desire to disempower and control women: overruling decisions is a public way to humiliate them. These researchers stress that both women and men can be bullies but unlike earlier workplace bullying researchers do not see this as indicating that gender is irrelevant. Instead they argue that:

> Organisational power relations are themselves heavily gendered – not in terms of the gender of the bodies that occupy managerial positions but in terms of the gendered nature of the discursive practices and assumptions that underpin the performance of management. (Simpson and Cohen, 2004:182)

Bray's research contributes data revealing that male and female bullies may adopt different bullying tactics in the context of gendered power relations in nursing. An interviewee described how a woman director of nursing bullied her by trying to wear her down, because 'that's what people who don't feel very powerful do. They develop other strategies for getting what they want which don't involve direct confrontation'; whereas a bullying male manager 'has his own sense of confidence ... [which is] probably a function of being male and having had the kinds of supports and feedback that are part of the network of power that is common with men' (p23). Bray ends her piece by saying that gender is not often discussed in workplace bullying research. Much more analysis of the gender dynamics of workplace bullying is needed.

Fox and Stallworth (2005) have explored racial bullying in the US, recognising that this is even less explored than gender dynamics. In the UK, Rayner *et al*, (2002:30) observe that less than 3 per cent of respondents to the Hoel and Cooper (2000) survey were from ethnic minorities. However, Quine's (2002) study of workplace bullying in UK healthcare indicated that Black and Asian junior doctors were more likely to encounter bullying than white doctors, showing a clear need for research in this area. Fox and Stallworth make a useful preliminary contribution, by explaining the dynamics of bullying experienced by Black men and women, but seek to differentiate between 'general bullying', which they say can happen to anyone and the 'racial/ethnic bullying' experienced by Black workers.

This research exploring gender and race issues in workplace bullying reveals some overlaps between sexual and racial harassment and bullying. One respondent in Simpson and Cohen's (2004) study was a woman academic who refused sexual advances from her line manager/PhD supervisor/mentor and was then bullied by him, abusing her verbally and appropriating her work. Thus, there are circumstances in which sexual harassment can lead to bullying. Samuels (2003:468) states that: 'the merging of the concepts of sexual harassment and bullying would be detrimental to women', because this 'makes it more difficult to deconstruct the relationship between the sexes and to understand the ways in which sexist attitudes are played out in the workplace'. Although analyses of the relevance of identity to workplace bullying are emerging, there is not yet a critical mass of research in this area. Samuels may still be correct in saying that the focus of bullying research makes particular analyses more difficult.

Fox and Stallworth's (2005) research also notes that bullying can include single incidents. This offers another illustration of how the workplace bullying discourse is developing beyond its early conceptualisations (see also Lee, 2000a), although this particular viewpoint is not yet widely accepted. Research in this area has also recently started to move beyond an exclusive focus upon bullying by superiors – and peers – in organisational hierarchies. In fact, Rayner *et al* (2002) say that looking at bullying by people who are not employees of a particular organisation (clients or customers, for example) is needed. Research which has already been conducted in this area includes the bullying of teachers by pupils in compulsory education.

Teacher targeted bullying

Teachers in compulsory education have always been made aware of their responsibilities in relation to pupil indiscipline (Munn, 1992).

Nevertheless, teacher responsibility for the conduct of pupils has recently been questioned in schools via differentiation between pupil indiscipline such as talking in class and what has now been identified as 'teacher targeted bullying' (TTB) such as mocking the teacher, saying 'you cannot control us' (Pervin and Turner, 1998:4). Pervin and Turner gave a questionnaire to 84 teachers at an inner-city UK school. Of the 39 male teachers and 45 female teachers who responded, 91 per cent indicated that they had encountered TTB in their careers. Pervin and Turner's study reveals that TTB has a detrimental effect upon staff morale and teacher performance, and implications for student learning. They rightly insist: 'it is important for management to listen and to take appropriate action. Teachers who suffer from TTB should not be simply dismissed as being incompetent. This approach to dealing with TTB will result in staff dissatisfaction and will also help condone this type of anti-social behaviour' (p7). Their study appears supportive of teachers who encounter TTB.

However, after reporting that nine per cent of staff said they accepted TTB as an unavoidable part of teaching, Pervin and Turner remark that 'this in-built acceptance of pupils bullying teachers needs to be challenged because *not all teachers are resilient enough* to ignore the negative effects' (p7 italics added). They assert that even if teachers have excellent understanding of their subjects and well developed teaching skills 'they *may not have the capacity* to stand up to certain pupils' (italics added). They recommend further studies to ascertain the characteristics of teachers susceptible to TTB and why some teachers escape it. Their article offers support, but at a price: they blame the victim. Teachers who are bullied by pupils are immediately seen as lacking in resilience and assertiveness.

This approach is replicated in a popular classroom management text read by teachers. In *Cracking the Hard Class* (2000), Rogers, an Australian teacher-educator, discusses 'teacher bullying'. He describes a male pupil perceiving in a woman teacher 'a weakness of character or personality that he could manipulate to his advantage' (Rogers, 2000:146). This way of conceptualising victims is consistent with the focus upon individuals which characterise traditional interpretations of workplace bullying. But it is even easier to claim that adult victims are responsible for their own misfortunes when the bullies are children, as Terry (1998) observes in his more positive interpretation of teachers. He points to the difficulties in studying teacher bullying by pupils because of 'over-simplified ideas about power relationships, and overly subjective and restrictive views about the nature of bullying' (Terry, 1998:256).

Terry's (1998) own small-scale research involved distributing questionnaires to 101 teachers at seven urban high schools in the north
Midlands of the UK, which drew a response rate of 30.06 per cent.
When asked if they had been bullied by a pupil or pupils in the pre-
ceding term, 56.4 per cent of respondents said that they had. When
asked how many of their colleagues had been bullied by pupils, 85.2
per cent knew of at least one. The bullying took the form of verbal
abuse (32.7 per cent), insolence (26.7 per cent), unacceptable name
calling (23.8 per cent) and deliberate and repetitive non-coopera-
tion (21.8 per cent).

> When asked if senior members of staff take incidents of bullying
> against teachers by their pupils seriously, 66.3 per cent responded
> with 'sometimes' or 'almost always'. Similarly, when asked if other
> colleagues took incidents of bullying against teachers by their
> pupils seriously, 75.1 per cent responded 'sometimes' or 'almost
> always'. (Terry, 1998:265-6)

This shows that co-workers and managers are not always unsupportive when staff are bullied by non-staff.

Terry reports that 51 per cent of teachers who said they had been
bullied by pupils 'reported that pupils may have viewed their actions
as bullying once or more that term' (p264). This research shows that
teachers, too, are culpable of bullying towards pupils. It concludes
that 'strategies may need to be incorporated into teacher training
schemes in order to pre-empt potential bully-abusive interactions,
and to bring into the mainstream of teacher perceptions the real
possibility of bully-abuse by pupils' (p266). Teachers definitely need
to know that bullying by pupils occurs and to consider anti-bullying
strategies. Far more important is Terry's recommendation that:

> A better understanding of the manner by which such abuse mani-
> fests itself, its widespread and insidious nature, and an acceptance
> by fellow professionals and others that such abuse is not simply a
> symptom of bad teaching but possibly a phenomenon of circum-
> stance must be a potential asset to the profession. It may be the
> case that good even talented teachers are being lost from the pro-
> fession due to the misconception that their teaching skills are at
> fault ... (p266)

Violence at work

Boyd (2002:155) argues that violence at work is a 'largely unrecog-
nised problem across all sectors' which has been highlighted in the
UK by research revealing 'the tripling of assaults on railway workers
during the period 1995-8'. Viitasara and Menckel (2002) note that

violence at work has traditionally been conceptualised as physical violence, yet non-physical abuse is increasingly located under this powerful umbrella term. As with workplace bullying research, the attributes of victims and perpetrators have been explored by researchers into violence at work and as in research into sexual harassment and bullying, the environment in which violence occurs has been considered.

The violence at work debate, in contrast to the workplace bullying debate, has always had a central focus upon violence perpetrated by non-employees. The Health and Safety Executive (HSE – the government agency which monitors work-related violence in the UK) (2004:1) states that: 'employees whose job requires them to deal with the public can be at risk from violence. Most at risk are those who are engaged in giving a service, caring, education, cash transactions, delivery/collection, controlling and representing authority'.

Hearn and Parkin (2001:65) observe that the discourse of physical violence 'is, like bullying, usually not specifically gendered...'. Nevertheless, there are indications of the development of a gender discourse in violence at work research. Boyd (2002), for instance, refers to a Trades Union Congress (TUC) survey conducted in 1999, which showed that 25-34 year-old women were the most likely targets of physical attacks and verbal violence. Liddle and Widdowson (1997) offer a ground-breaking analysis of gender and violence at work, which draws upon qualitative data gathered in a welfare benefits office. They reveal that men and women claimants deployed a 'vocabulary of sexual denigration such as 'slag', 'whore' and 'bitch' when making verbal attacks on women workers' (p40) and they stress that verbal abuse from male claimants was taken more seriously than verbal abuse from female claimants because it was more likely to escalate into physical violence.

Violence at work research involves a recognition of how client violence creates particular difficulties for professional employees. Whitehead (2003), for instance, focuses upon violence in occupational therapy in the UK. One of Whitehead's interviewees explains that when she was physically attacked by a patient:

> My initial feeling was just to, to get out of there and just not be in that situation ... but I felt like, you know, what is my role here, what's my job, what am I supposed to be doing in this situation? And I was thinking about supporting my other member of staff and also about the other clients who were there. (p96)

Whitehead reports that respondents thought they would have responded differently if not in a work setting. This is because the Code of Ethics and Professional Conduct for Occupational Therapists reminds workers that they should not cause distress to a client.

Secker *et al* (2004) observed that healthcare professionals do not always put the patient first. They studied an acute admissions unit in a UK psychiatric hospital for five months and discuss eleven incidents of physical and verbal violence that occurred. Three incidents were understood to be due to the client's mental illness. They interpret the other nine as power struggles between clients and staff. The authors remark that 'a striking theme in relation to these power struggles was the apparent inability of staff to look at what was happening from the client's perspective' (p175). They continue: 'had the staff on duty been able to respond to clients' agitation or distress, this might have avoided what appeared to be an inevitable escalation culminating in the management of all but one client by control and restraint, followed by the administration of intramuscular medication'. The researchers found that debriefing after the incidents was rare, but in the little there was 'the overriding aim appeared to have been to correct the client's behaviour, rather than exploring what had happened from the client's perspective or considering together how it might have been avoided' (p176).

While Secker *et al* imply that violence is always the consequence of staff non-empathy with patients, Aitken and Noble (2001), reflecting specifically upon the treatment of women in secure settings, present a more balanced picture. But they agree that 'the most consistently profound violence ... is a lack of internalisation, empathy or engagement with a woman's reality by care staff' (p81), while stressing that many workers do not behave in this way. And they draw attention to nurses' experiences of stress-related absences, and the expansion of roles they are expected to fulfil.

Annandale's (1996) study of risk culture in nursing is useful as it explains the circumstances in which UK healthcare professionals are working. She refers to the emphasis upon individual accountability in nursing and notes that while there is an emphasis upon partnership with patients, 'consumerism still seems to have the effect of pitting patient and provider against each other' (p427). Nurses 'appreciate why patients want to know more and question more', yet 'they can also experience the informed patient as a threat' (p432). Annandale argues that defensive practices are 'in the interests of neither nurses ... nor patients' (p416). Aitken and Noble

(2001:79) make the important point that: 'in many ways, the system violates and is violent to all within it'.

In compulsory education, Blaya (2003:650) says that teachers in 'every country [feel that] ... the teaching profession is becoming increasingly hazardous'. The author surveyed nearly 500 teachers in schools in England and France to assess working conditions in the two countries, with particular reference to school violence. She reports that 'more than half of the adult respondents report having difficult relationships with the pupils and only .4 per cent estimate that they are extremely good' (Blaya, 2003:654). The *Times Educational Supplement* reports that: 'the number of teachers in England who had to take at least three days off work because of attacks [by pupils] increased from 205 in 2003 to 272 in 2004'. A spokesperson for the Liberal Democrats remarks that: 'it is utterly appalling and totally unacceptable that teachers face this level of serious violence in school' (Shaw, 2005:2). This coverage seems to be sympathetic to teachers.

However, in the same issue, we find an article entitled: 'Ill-prepared to cope with the 'classroom yobs'', reporting that a survey by the Teacher Training Agency reveals that 'a third of new teachers say that they are not well enough trained to control badly-behaved pupils' (Paton and Seth, 2005:4). Thus, like early explorations of the sexual harassment of women teachers and pupils by school boys (Whitbread, 1989), violence in schools is often reduced to a problem of teacher inexperience. However, Blaya (2003:666), in contrast with Lahelma *et al*'s (2000) study of the sexual harassment of teachers, states that teachers are 'not solely responsible for the school culture and climate in which they work'. She calls for 'in-depth training of management staff as well as supervision and administrative employees, for all members of the educational community are affected by violence when it occurs'. She does not indicate whether managers welcome this idea.

What must be recognised here, as with the points made with reference to the NHS, is the context in which teachers in the UK are working. As Wragg *et al* (2000) observe, accountability in compulsory education has been increasing since the 1980s. They describe the current situation as one of 'high accountability [and] low trust' (p13).

As we have seen, 'violence' is no longer just taken to refer to physical violence. Waddington *et al* (2005:158) remark that this inclusive definition 'respects ... diversity of experience', but are concerned that an inclusive definition can become 'so broad that almost any situation that any person finds disagreeable can be described as a form of 'violence'. Focusing specifically upon professional employees and their encounters with patients, clients and suspects, they argue that inclusive definitions can make professionals unaccountable. They note that because researchers of violence rarely interview more than one party involved in a particular incident, they risk 'accepting uncritically ... a partial response' (Waddington *et al*, 2005:147). They propose that 'describing incidents as 'conflicts' or 'disputes' might avoid the implicit attribution of blame without diminishing the quality of the experience for those involved'. Clearly, the way in which we describe unacceptable conduct towards professionals is important. Conceptualisations of unacceptable student conduct towards academics are considered throughout this book.

Discussion

This chapter offers a feminist sociological exploration of the sexual harassment, workplace bullying and violence at work debates. The traditional conceptualisation of sexual harassment: white, heterosexual women's experiences of unwanted male sexual conduct in the workplace, reveals that victim-blaming is not a convincing explanation for sexual harassment. The rethinking sexual harassment debate presented demonstrates the highly reflective nature of the discourse. An analysis of inappropriate client sexual behaviour, patients who act provokingly, and contrapower sexual harassment in healthcare and compulsory education followed. It showed the unease often – but not always (Robinson, 2000) – displayed by researchers when the victims of unwanted male sexual conduct are professional women mistreated by non-staff. Researcher unease with victims of unwanted sexual conduct is highly problematic because women still routinely blame themselves when they have encountered sexual harassment (Hinze, 2004). They certainly do not need researchers to contribute to this process of self-blame.

Workplace bullying, a newer concept, traditionally involves workers being mistreated by their superiors or peers in organisational hierarchies. In contrast to the sexual harassment discourse, workplace bullying research tends to provide rather unsympathetic profiles of workplace bullying victims, which can be interpreted as victim-blaming – but there are exceptions. Terry's (1998) study of teacher bullying is exemplary in working towards ensuring dignity and respect in the workplace. Research which has shifted away from a fascination with the personalities of victims and perpetrators is to be welcomed.

Finally, the violence at work debate has always maintained that violence can be perpetrated by non-employees. The inclusive nature of what counts as violence may be problematic compared with the generally more discrete conceptualisations of workplace sexual harassment and bullying. Violence research, like analyses of workplace bullying, has yet to recognise in a consistent and clear way how aspects of people's identities are relevant to workplace experiences. Despite the recognition that non-employees can be violent towards employees, victim-blaming is still going on in this field of research.

Unease about non-employees mistreating employees is present in many studies of this manifestation of sexual harassment, bullying and violence at work. Hadjifotiou (1983:13) suggests that 'because of the control which a supervisor exercises over a worker's job prospects, harassment from a superior was usually viewed more seriously'. Professional men and women in occupations such as healthcare and education are not responded to effectively when they are mistreated by non-employees because they are expected to show a: 'sensitive and responsive approach to people's needs' (Hadjifotiou, 1983:44).

The perpetrators of sexual harassment, bullying and violence in healthcare and compulsory education are usually seen either as too unwell or too young to know what they are doing: this is part of the reason for the unease. The extensive research in these areas is likely to have an influence elsewhere. And whilst healthcare professionals are recognised as being in highly stressful jobs, academia is seen as 'a liberal, democratic institution that fosters equality and enlightenment' (Grauerholz, 1996:29), a pleasant place of employment. Collins and Parry-Jones (2000:771) refer to the stereotype of the academic as: 'a fortunate person who does not 'get their hands dirty', plays with theory, reads, writes, enjoys long lunch hours, late starts, early finishes and long holidays'. Analysis of unacceptable student conduct towards academics must therefore proceed carefully, and the nature of the context in which problems occur must be noted.

Chapter Two takes further the issue that unacceptable conduct towards a professional employee by a non-employee is often interpreted as a consequence of the inexperience of the professional employee and challenges this individual pathology approach to victimisation.

2

It's just a matter
of inexperience...

This chapter introduces the problem of students behaving badly in UK higher education (HE), through interviews with women graduate teaching assistants and early career academics. I have chosen to start with them because of the common views that it is only inexperienced academics who have problems with students, and that these problems are generally caused by their inexperience.

These views are underpinned by models of how university teachers develop: Nyquist and Wulff (1996, cited in Sharpe, 2000) assert that teachers encounter three stages of development. First, they wonder if students will like them. Sharpe (2000:134) explains this as teachers 'not feeling very different from being a student themselves'. Second, they question their teaching skills: they wonder if they will be able to maintain discipline. By this stage, teachers, Sharpe says, are beginning to differentiate themselves from students. The final stage of teacher development involves wondering whether students are learning: they 'start to develop professional tutor/learner relationships with their students without taking their behaviour too personally' (p134).

Brown (2001) provides an example of this way of thinking in practice. She relates how when she was a new, untrained teacher, her students kept arriving late and talking in class, which made her feel undermined. As the disruption persisted, she 'was now dreading lectures ... perhaps I should even begin to think about changing jobs' (p22). Her response is precisely the one most new academics are encouraged to make: she immediately takes personal responsibility for what has happened. She says: 'students can find countless ways to disrupt lectures, some intentional and some not, and being able to cope with what the situation throws up is all part of developing the confidence one needs to be a lecturer' (p26).

Contrary to conventional wisdom in academia, under-developed teaching is not necessarily the reason for unacceptable student conduct and even if the teacher is inexperienced, the answer to the problem of unacceptable student conduct is not simply for teachers to develop more confidence via staff development learning and teaching courses. This approach would simply parallel inappropriate responses to unacceptable conduct towards healthcare and education professionals as discussed in Chapter One. Instead, a different interpretation needs to be considered. Later in the same piece, Brown makes a more realistic observation that: 'having disruptive students in a class is not necessarily a reflection on the lecturer, but can be just a fact of life' (p26). Disappointingly, she does not develop this point. Leonard (2001:211) in a woman's guide to doctoral studies, briefly but importantly notes that 'women research students may get harassed by other research students, by porters or lab technicians, and by undergraduate students [they] are teaching'. However, Brown's sound premise that unacceptable student conduct is 'not necessarily a reflection on the lecturer' does not mean that unacceptable student conduct should be seen as 'a fact of life' (Brown, 2001:26). A more sophisticated interpretation is required, developing Leonard's recognition that university students can mistreat their teachers. I suggest that a more sophisticated interpretation of unacceptable student conduct needs to examine the reasons why students behave badly towards graduate teaching assistants and early career academics and consider how they might respond.

This book shows that it is not only inexperienced teachers who encounter unacceptable student conduct. It describes the unacceptable student conduct encountered by more experienced academics, women and men, and relates these experiences to individual identities because, as Bhopal (2002:111) remarks: 'little research has explored the ways in which ... identity ... affect[s] ... experiences of teaching and learning in higher education'. I also reflect upon ways of conceptualising unacceptable student conduct, for instance, as contrapower sexual harassment, sexism, bullying and violence. The interpretation 'unacceptable student conduct' is used as the starting point for exploration of staff-student problems.

The experiences recounted by two young female graduate teaching assistants are analysed below. Eve is a white, single 25 year-old with no children, a graduate teaching assistant at a pre-1992 university Business School, who was harangued by a mature woman student in the first seminar she facilitated. Alison is a white, single 25 year-old with no children, a graduate teaching assistant in a Politics Subject Area at a post-1992 university, who was the subject of persistent rumours spread by four women mature students. Then two women early career academics are considered: Emily, a white, married, 29 year-old with no children, a Lecturer in Sociology at a pre-1992 university, who was physically attacked by a young male undergraduate student, and stalked/sexually harassed by another young male undergraduate student and Rachel, a white, married, 32 year-old with no children, a former Lecturer in History at a pre-1992 university, who encountered a complaint from a young woman whose dissertation she supervised. None of these women was disabled.

All four cases reveal aspects of academic women's experiences of unacceptable student conduct. All the graduate teaching assistants and early career academics interviewed for this research were also women. The experiences of abuse by students of male graduate teaching assistants and early career academics remain to be explored elsewhere, although the experiences of a newly-appointed but quite experienced male academic are considered in Chapter Five.

The analysis provided here is relevant not just to graduate teaching assistants and early career academics but also to many individuals who teach part-time in UK higher education because it shows that academic status is implicated in student misconduct towards teachers. Research completed by Abbas and McLean (2001) has revealed that part-time teachers feel undermined in front of students because they are not entitled to physical space. One part-time teacher remarked: 'the image we project to the students isn't good because we're all walking round with bags and they look on us as not proper teachers'. Another concurred, saying: 'I think that's part of the problem with this guy [a student]. He doesn't see me as any kind of lecturer or anything else'. And a third added: 'You have no status; you haven't got an office, you haven't got your name on a door' (Abbas and McLean, 2001:347).

Eve: 'I stayed because I needed the money'

At the time of our interview, Eve was a final year PhD student and graduate teaching assistant. Leonard (2001:137) observes that graduate teaching assistantships are a way for 'universities to attract good candidates who otherwise couldn't afford to do a PhD and it may be easier to get appointed to such a job than to get a research council grant', yet she also notes that 'with the massification and marketisation of higher education, it is more often a way to get ... cheap, casual teaching, often with minimal support for the workers and little concern for their career development'. Eve's experiences seem to offer an illustration of the latter conceptualisation of the graduate teaching assistant.

Departmental politics, such as battles concerning access to the photocopier, had undermined Eve's enjoyment of academic life over the last three years. Consequently, she was not sure whether or not she wished to apply for jobs in academia. While these are clearly not the only reasons for Eve's ambivalence, the events analysed here have significantly affected how she views university teaching at this early stage in her academic career.

When she was in her first year as a graduate teaching assistant she was required to facilitate seminars for twenty postgraduate students who had attended lectures delivered by an eminent professor. Graduate teaching assistants are often considered to benefit students' learning because they are close in age and experience to their students (Sharpe, 2000), but Eve was in a difficult situation. She was younger and less experienced than her students, had no training as a teacher and was not entirely sure what was expected of her as a seminar tutor. A problem arose in the first session:

> We got into the classroom and one of the students – I could tell that she was a bit annoyed beforehand – stood up in the classroom and started shouting at me saying: 'It's your responsibility! You're going to sort it out! That lecturer is dreadful! What are you going to do about it?' She was being quite aggressive, I thought, and quite un-necessarily so. I was completely thrown.

Eve reflected upon why she thought the woman student, Angela, had behaved this way. She felt that Angela, being a mature student entering part-time postgraduate education concurrent with a successful professional career, was not prepared to countenance what she immediately perceived as 'poor service' from the eminent professor. The notion of a student receiving poor service from an academic is illustrative of the student-as-consumer (explored in Chapter

Three). The professor's style, Eve said, 'did take a bit of getting used to, but it's certainly worth getting used to, he's a man with a lot of knowledge'. Yet the problem for Eve was not simply Angela's hasty perception of his lecture. She felt bullied by Angela:

> I don't think she liked there being me, somebody who is probably twenty years younger than her, in authority over her. A big part of me thought that she was deliberately trying to throw me. And I have to say that she succeeded really well. I did not know how to handle it. I felt that I just didn't have the competency to deal with that. I remember standing in front of the class of twenty students from, you know, all different countries, different ages etc and my mouth opening and closing, face very red and just not knowing quite what I should answer to her. I think in the end I tried to be calm and said 'Right, I'll go through the lecture material'.

After the class, Angela went to Eve's office: 'she said she hadn't meant it as a personal thing towards me, but the lecturer was appalling and what was I going to do about it? Still very, very demanding of me, and I really didn't know what to do at all'. Subsequently, Eve told the eminent professor what had happened. He was amused and advised Eve to refer Angela to him if further problems occurred. Eve remained concerned, however, that a mature woman student preferred to harangue her, a young PhD student facilitating a seminar, rather than approach a strongly established member of staff. Carson (2001) observes that younger women staff can encounter problems with students because 'they are not thought to carry the weight and authority of male colleagues' (p342). Eve felt she had been disadvantaged and remained disadvantaged because she had not been trained to teach and was therefore not sure how to respond to an irate student:

> I certainly wish somebody had pointed it out to me that it [a problem in the classroom] might happen and if something did happen, there would be some support for me afterwards or I would not be the first person it had happened to as a postgraduate student, but because it happened very early on in my teaching, I was totally unprepared. It showed in the way that I dealt with it, which was not very well.

Eve clearly felt that she should not have been asked to teach a class before having any staff development in learning and teaching. Blaxter *et al* (1998:82) observe that: 'for many academics, regardless of whether they have had any specific training, their initial experiences of teaching are rather daunting' and remark that published accounts of early teaching experiences reflect: 'a mixture of surprise, horror and loneliness'. So Eve would not have been adequately prepared for what happened to her even if she had undertaken training for teaching.

Much more important is Eve's point that she would anticipate support if problems occurred in the classroom. The eminent professor's amused response when Eve reported the incident to him was hardly support: he stressed his own lack of concern that a complaint had been made, not appreciating how a young graduate teaching assistant must have felt when a student started shouting. His response illustrates how unacceptable student conduct can be viewed with incomprehension by those who have not or do not believe they have encountered it themselves but hear only second-hand accounts of such experiences. Eve received support from a newly-appointed male lecturer 'who was teaching the same students and had some problems with Angela as well'.

The next term, Eve's examination paper was mislaid by a secretary, and Eve had to rush to the examination room with copies of the paper. Afterwards, 'I sent the students an email to apologise for what happened. I didn't wish to assign any blame, so they assumed it had been our error [Eve was teaching this class with another doctoral student]'. A student made a complaint. Subsequently, the Head of Department emailed all the students stressing that the problem had been administrative, but Eve said: 'I wasn't convinced the students fully believed that'.

Shortly after this second incident of difficulties with students, Eve attended a three-day training course for postgraduate teachers, which was, she said, 'too little too late'. The course seemed to imply that only certain sorts of problems would be presented by students and that these problems could be easily resolved, so she felt that 'it didn't deal with the practicalities... I realised it didn't happen like that. I didn't have any sort of feeling that I had acquired any general skills to go and deal with situations'. Clearly, a three-day course was insufficient to cover all of the topics Eve wanted to explore. As she had already encountered unacceptable student conduct, she realised that 'dealing with difficult students' training can be quite simplistic. More effective staff development is discussed in Chapter Six.

As she has gained experience of teaching over the last three years, Eve feels that she has 'relaxed a little bit', but she said: 'I'm not sure that I have gained much more confidence in my ability to teach and to teach well. I've looked at what makes a good teacher, but I'm not sure I'm good at it because my confidence was knocked very early on.' Eve indicated that she remained teaching the class after being harangued only because she needed the money and said that she: 'spent the whole of the first term teaching with my back rigid because I was so stressed about it. I was very, very miserable.'

Readers might have expected a more 'shocking' first example of unacceptable student conduct in higher education. They might even be surprised that Eve was so badly affected by a student shouting and felt blamed by students for an administrative error. They might view her case much as Drysdale interprets her first encounter with instances of workplace bullying. Drysdale in Adams (1992:4) says that she felt 'irritated' when Anne, a bank employee, 'recounted how her manager had ridiculed her in front of the others for her vegetarian eating habits. Her response at once suggested that Anne must be over-sensitive. Did she really have to resort to eating her lunch in the ladies' loo to escape his taunts?'. For Drysdale, Anne's account of workplace bullying becomes important when it transpires that her fellow employees are similarly affected. In Eve's account, the fact that students have behaved inappropriately and unfairly are what is important. These experiences are rendered even more problematic for Eve by the stage she is at in her career.

If we review the events, we can see just why the experience is particularly undermining for Eve, a young PhD student and graduate teaching assistant, not well briefed and placed in front of a class of mature, post-experience MA students just after she has completed her own MA. The professor with whom she is working has a style not all the students like and which one student, much older than Eve, is not willing to work with. Rather than approaching the professor privately for guidance, she chooses to complain loudly in front of Eve's seminar group. The rest of the group remain silent. Eve is unaccustomed to twenty pairs of eyes watching her every move and to a student shouting at her. If she agrees with the student she will be undermining a senior colleague. If she disagrees, the shouting may intensify.

Moreover, teachers often feel they should not object to what students have said: Tutors A and B (1996:9) note that 'tutors aren't allowed to tell students off'. The situation might have come to the attention of managers in the Business School, and Eve might have been classed as a poor teacher by the end of her first class. As Abbas and McLean (2001:347) observe, part-time staff often: 'take care not to indicate problems either with their own practice or with senior colleagues for fear of jeopardising future chances'. Eventually, Eve manages to respond and restore order, but she cannot congratulate herself because doing so took time and she feels she lost face in front of the students. This is all far from pleasant in the short term. In the medium and perhaps even long term, she has to overcome the memory of the first few minutes of her first seminar every time she enters a classroom. It is not surprising that she has been slow to enjoy teaching and is still unsure whether she teaches well. And when students later complained when the examination paper was mislaid, her unease with teaching was reinforced. It is evident that: 'in graduate school, women have reported lower levels of academic self-concept, more negative self-concepts and less career commitment than men' (Ulku-Steiner *et al*, 2000, cited in Barata *et al*, 2005: 239): graduate school is clearly a difficult experience for women, even without unacceptable conduct from students.

Alison: 'I need a break or I am going to go mad!'

Alison was a final year PhD student and graduate teaching assistant at the time of our interview. She reflected upon experiences which began in her first year as a graduate teaching assistant, three years earlier. She had been facilitating seminars with six students: three mature women, two younger women and a mature male student. Students were to be assessed via their contributions to these seminars. Alison recollected:

> [The mature male student's] seminar skills were just fantastic ... [he had] all the skills that I was looking for. ... There was a small contingent of women who didn't like the fact that he did well and rather than take on board the kind of formative feedback that I had given them, about what they needed to do to improve, their first response was that this was some sort of favouritism because he was a man.

One of the younger women students informed Alison that the three mature women students believed she was favouring the mature male student and that they 'were going to take out an official complaint because he is doing well'. They were implying that Alison was giving the man extra help, which was untrue, and anyway she had already said to every member of the group that 'if you want extra help on how to improve, come and see me'.

Alison felt that her youth was relevant to the women students: 'you know, 'how can she assess us when she's got no idea of life, blah, blah, blah''. Equally, she felt that her status as a PhD student was problematic: 'it's just like, well, they don't know what they're talking

32

about yet'. The women started spreading the rumour that Alison had done badly in her first degree and MA programme and that: 'that's why I was so horrible to them, because they were more intelligent'.

Alison contacted her woman line manager, the Head of Politics, with whom she had a good work relationship. The Head was very supportive: she called the three students in and told them in Alison's presence that: 'this is what we've heard. We're not happy with it. If you want to make an official complaint, do it, but you'll lose.' The three women gave a verbal assurance that this was the end of the matter, but when Alison left her line manager's office 'they were still in the corridor, still saying the same sort of things: 'this is the university covering it up''.

The year progressed with the women students repeatedly accusing Alison of favouritism. Alison found seminars 'horrible'. The three women would not make eye contact with her or the rest of the group and she felt she 'never knew where I was going to be attacked next and I was waiting for them to try to probe into my personal life and stuff like that'. The Head of Politics would have been happy for Alison to take out a grievance against the students because of their persistent misconduct towards her, and told her: 'this is harassment, do you want to make a complaint? We'll back you'. This is a rare instance of unconditional support from a line manager for an academic encountering unacceptable student conduct: we see no further examples until Chapter Five. Alison was also supported by a fellow doctoral student and a newly-appointed lecturer:

> [The doctoral student] started his PhD at the same time as me, and we talked quite a lot because he'd had a difficult seminar group ... so we spent quite a lot of time over coffee bitching about how terrible it was. And there was a lecturer who had completed his PhD the year I started who was very, very supportive and gave me the right advice at the time, which was 'just forget about it, it's not your problem, it's theirs, just get on with your job and do it well', but at the time I just couldn't take that on board.

Alison did not choose to pursue a grievance because she felt it would be unfair to the staff of the subject area. And she felt that if she did complain, the three women would see themselves as victims and: 'I didn't want to give them that power.'

The next academic year Alison was asked to teach second-year classes. The Head of Politics reminded the three trouble makers that their conduct towards Alison should not be repeated this year, after which she went off sick. Alison found herself taking more and more responsibility for the small specialist Politics degree. One of the three students remained very hostile, unfairly accusing Alison of failing to recognise that personal difficulties were affecting her academic work, after Alison had negotiated extended deadlines for her.

At the time of the interview in Alison's third year at the university, the rumours had stopped: 'because everyone on the course knows who I am, how I operate and I think they respect me for what I do ... Someone started up with those comments again at the beginning of this year, and the rest of the group jumped on them and said 'we've had enough of this'.' Alison should not have needed to prove herself in this way, but the requirement for academic women to earn the respect of students prevails, as shown by Carson (2001): students view male lecturers as 'automatically worthy of respect', whereas they 'regard women teachers as less estimable and authoritative than their male counterparts' (p341). Alison's case illustrates that the lack of respect for women academics noted by Carson is heightened when the woman academic is a young graduate teaching assistant.

Unlike Eve, Alison had successfully completed a short teaching course before she encountered unacceptable student conduct. This underlines the point made at the start of this chapter, that sending academics onto teaching courses is not necessarily the answer to the problem of unacceptable student conduct. In Alison's case, successful completion of the teaching course in fact affected her teaching confidence when she encountered unacceptable student conduct: she felt she had developed skills in learning and teaching and always reflected upon her practice, yet she was still encountering problems with students. She said:

> My confidence just went completely, and it took quite a long time for it to come back. I suppose it's only this year I've got the confidence and strength back to say this isn't about me, this is things going on in their lives. One of the students has apologised to me, completely unprovoked, to say that there were things going on in her personal life, and she was sorry she took it out on me.

This echoes Eve's unhappiness in the classroom after she was harangued by a student. Thus encountering unacceptable student conduct at an early point in an academic career is clearly highly problematic in terms of the development of the confidence required of a university teacher (Brown, 2001).

Alison now believes she was bullied by the three students. She reflected upon her experiences at school and decided that 'having experienced bullying at school and experiencing [this situation at work] it was just the same, it works in the same way'. She said that when the problem first arose she found it difficult to recognise it as bullying: 'because I firmly thought that saying I was being bullied by these students was a bit weak. You know, they're students and I was being employed to do this and, you know, how could they bully me?' This is typical of how academics are encouraged to view their experiences of unacceptable student conduct and it parallels how professionals in other fields often view problematic interactions with clients. Alison's experience clearly shows that this is a simplistic view, which she eventually dismissed.

Alison decided not to apply for academic jobs in her final year as a graduate teaching assistant. She said: 'I need a break or I am going to go mad!'. Instead, she found an opening in political activism. She chose this route partly because she felt she wanted to return to this area in which she had worked before and 'partly because the PhD process was so intense'. Alison felt that had she not encountered the problems described here she would have focused upon finding a full-time lectureship, although she intends to return to academia in a few years time. I wonder whether she will, not just because she may reflect upon these experiences and decide that she is unwilling to repeat them but because of the highly competitive nature of academia.

Emily: 'I'm moving towards not caring as much ...'

Emily, an early career academic, explained that her difficulties began when Tom, a young male student, enrolled for an option she was teaching. She explained that Tom was persistently late for classes:

> And when I'd try to address this, whether privately or in the seminar room itself, he would just make a comment along the lines of 'well, I try as hard as I can but it's not that interesting, so why would I get up for it?'. He would talk while I was speaking all the time. The funny thing is that he wasn't actually undermining what I was saying, critiquing what I was saying, he was just really seeing the seminar as a very social place. He was good looking, had a lot of presence and had four or five women students who liked him and they would sit and giggle at what he was saying. He was very disruptive in that way, and when I tried to call a halt to that he would roll his eyes and sigh loudly. You know, a continuous level of disruption in the class.

Tom proceeded not to attend assessed presentations or complete online preparation materials. Emily said: 'I was trying to give him help, thinking he just didn't know how to use the material. And he turned and walked out of the class when I was speaking to him one-to-one.' After a while Tom stopped attending classes.

Emily recognised what she was experiencing: 'I think it was bullying … because I felt out of control and I felt like I didn't want to go to the classroom, like I didn't want to see him, I didn't want to see him in the corridor'. She was particularly undermined by the fact that: 'I would be speaking in class and he would just be speaking to these women at the front and it was like I didn't exist, so [it was] that exclusion tactic that I think bullying does, demeaning you, like you're not even worth paying attention to'.

Although aware that she was encountering bullying, unlike Alison, Emily first reported Tom, in line with university procedures, when he began failing to meet the requirement to attend classes. She did not take action when Tom was being disrespectful in class. She knew she could take action in response to student non-attendance at classes but was not sure whether she could object to student disrespect in class. The need for clear university procedures with regard to unacceptable student conduct is stressed in Chapter Six.

Emily next saw Tom at an evening seminar. After it she explained that she had put him forward for a warning because his attendance was unsatisfactory. A warning is a serious matter at Emily's university: after two warnings in an academic year a student would be expelled, although Emily had never heard of this actually happening. She recalled:

> There was no one left in the seminar room and he began shouting at me, 'did I know who his father was?' and 'his father would be outraged that I was going to do this to him'. I kept trying to calm the situation down, saying, 'this is your first year, you've got time to make up for this', but he kept shouting and shouting, and shouting even more. I became increasingly uncomfortable as I began to realise that even the porters were probably not still in the vicinity. And he came at me. He's a big, athletic chap. And he grabbed me by the shoulders and was shaking me and shoving me. So I grabbed a chair and kind of manoeuvred away from him and put it between us and shouted back that 'you have to get a grip, don't do this, or you will be expelled immediately' – which I didn't know was true or not. And he left the room shouting threats and obscenities at me, how his father would see that I would lose my job. I was shaking when I got out of the room and had to walk home. I had to walk home in the dark. Do you know, it was ridiculous, but I thought he's going to wait outside for me and have another go at me.

Emily never considered calling the police to report this physical attack, even though she would have been perfectly within her rights to do so. Instead, she decided to raise the matter at the School Board of Studies, a meeting at which every student's social and intellectual development is considered. This meeting was to take place later the same week.

Emily was taken aback by the response she received at School Board. She explained that after a twenty minute discussion, Tom had been issued with a warning. Emily told me: 'They were very concerned that he didn't get expelled because he might cause problems. As far as I was concerned he had done enough to just get expelled.' Emily felt aggrieved that a warning had not been issued instantly. Emily's co-workers responded badly too. Immediately before the meeting, she mentioned the incident to a group of male co-workers:

> One of them in particular laughed and said 'he is a bit of a jerk' and that was it. It was that physical fear when I left the seminar room and was worried that he was going to be outside. And this man was just laughing and saying 'he's a bit of a jerk'. Well, he's not 'a bit of a jerk' actually, he's really deeply problematic. And, at School Board, two male colleagues felt that I was overreacting.

Women co-workers were informally supportive outside the meeting, saying: "gosh that would be really terrible. Gosh that would be awful'. A lot of commiseration, but when it came down to formal procedure, no, there's no back-up'. Emily said that what happened, 'made me question the purpose of School Board and the school's disciplinary procedures, if someone like that, who is obviously deeply problematic, can just slip through for whatever reason'. It is quite clear that university managers and fellow academics at the School Board of Studies responded irresponsibly to Emily's experience of a physical attack.

The second problem Emily recounted started in a first year undergraduate class and involved a different student, Joe. He had to submit either an answer to a set question or a more personal essay. Joe's personal essay became:

> more and more personal, nothing to do with me, and I began to worry that he was quite unstable and I thought he needed to go for counselling. And obviously because he was writing the essay for me to see, I thought he was asking me to do something, so I did make more of an effort to draw him out. He began coming to my office hours a lot. He came pretty much every week. He always had a good reason to come.

Emily had previously had a woman undergraduate who wrote that she was suicidal and Emily had helped her to seek counselling. She assumed that this was a similar situation but this was not necessarily the case.

When teaching ended for the year, Emily began to see Joe regularly in the city centre, at cafes she frequented with her husband and friends. She said: 'he would come up and sit down ... and would say 'hi, how are you?' and he'd spend the evening. So I was still thinking 'oh he's just being kind of clingy''. Then Joe went abroad for a holiday and kept sending Emily letters and postcards. She recalled: 'I was feeling increasingly uncomfortable, because I didn't know what I could do about it, because he was no longer my student.'

Joe returned from his holidays and caught up with Emily and her husband in a pub: 'my husband went for drinks and Joe really started slagging off my husband. He works at the university. Joe knew that. I kind of really put him in his place. And my husband and I left.' This was a significant moment in Emily's interactions with Joe. So far, we have seen Joe seeming to entertain views of Emily as girlfriend material. When she strongly identified herself as married by supporting her husband, Joe stopped being 'clingy'. Instead, Emily began receiving silent phone calls at home. She said: 'I had no idea if it was Joe, but it started happening almost as soon as he was in the pub and I told him off.' Emily arranged for her number to be changed and made ex-directory. When the new term started, Emily began to receive anonymous emails at work, 'telling me how he thought I was really sexy'. At first, Emily believed this was just anonymous spam email:

> Then I began really reading them. I was getting them two or three times a week, and then he began telling me what clothes I was wearing, especially to lectures. The first year is big, 200 students, and I was lecturing and I saw Joe at the back of the theatre. There's no reason why he should have been there.

Emily did not know what to do because she could not prove that Joe was the anonymous caller or emailer. Then: 'I got a phone call at 3am, and I picked it up half asleep and it was Joe. He said: 'I want to love you so much'. I said 'what?' And he said; 'I want to love you so much'. Emily hung up. The next morning she went to see the undergraduate secretary. The two women composed an email: 'saying this was inappropriate and she made vague threats to him that couldn't actually be followed through because he wasn't my student. Then it stopped immediately'.

At School Board of Studies Joe was mentioned by one of Emily's co-workers for not attending classes. Emily said: 'I just want to raise this issue that he became quite fixated on me, to the point where I felt harassed in my own home', to which the Head of School replied: 'you should have come and told me immediately when it started happening'. Emily said that the situation had built up gradually but if it happened again she would approach her at once. But the Head of School insisted: 'No, it's really, really, not on that you didn't come and see me immediately'. Emily said: 'so again I was like ... what's happening here? Again I apologised. It was noted in the minutes that he had harassed a member of staff.'

Emily had reported being sexually harassed by a student and yet it was she who was reprimanded, not the student. Perhaps the Head of School was annoyed because if Emily had approached her she would have attempted to resolve the matter and she had been denied this opportunity. However, Emily's treatment at the earlier School Board, when she had been physically attacked by a student, suggests that support would not necessarily have been available. Emily was still having problems with Joe at the time of our interview: she had recently discovered that Joe was spreading rumours that they had had an affair. Emily told me: 'I don't want to make a big deal about it because ... I'd just prefer it to go away'.

When I asked Emily how these incidents had affected her views of academia, she replied:

> I'm moving towards not caring as much. When [students] kind of give you their line of crap, I'm much more wanting to cut to the chase with them rather than ... I've talked to other female colleagues about it, whether it's kind of a female thing to want to have your students be OK ... but I'm moving away from that. Whether it's because of these incidents or not, I don't know, or whether I'm becoming tired of doing it.

Emily said that: 'I really love teaching, and at the time [when the first situation arose] it was the first time I was worried about going into a class, just in the sense that I couldn't plan the class out, I didn't know what he might do'. She reflected: 'I don't think it's undermined my confidence, but it's made me not like it [teaching] as much'. It is early in Emily's career for her view of staff-student interaction to have become jaded and her enjoyment of university teaching diminished. Clearly, early experiences of unacceptable student conduct and inappropriate managerial intervention adversely affect academic careers. Unlike Eve and Alison, Emily had a couple of years experience of enjoying the role of university teacher before the students' abuse, so she retained her confidence despite severely damaging experiences.

Rachel: 'I think the only way is not to care, but I don't think there are many of us who can do that'

Rachel had resigned from her job as Lecturer in History by the time I interviewed her. Two years before, close to the start of her career as a lecturer, Rachel had encountered a problem with a third-year dissertation student, Sharon, whom she had informed that her draft chapters were at the level of a lower second and had given detailed feedback to help her improve. She intended to be helpful, particularly as Sharon had said she wanted to achieve a first class degree. At the end of the autumn term, students were required to write a mid-course evaluation of their supervisors. Rachel recalled:

> I found this [evaluation] which basically told lies about me. Sharon had said I had lost a computer disk containing two draft chapters and she'd had to do the work again, which was not true and quite a few other things – I hadn't got time for her, I hadn't given her the support she needed. I'd actually seen her more times than any of my other students. I saw her for about an hour every fortnight which I definitely consider to be enough – and that was excluding corridor meetings and emails.

Rachel had judged Sharon's draft chapters as meriting a lower second, not the wanted first class. Shevlin *et al* (2000:398) observe that there is 'a positive association between expected grades and ratings of teaching effectiveness', which may account for Sharon's evaluation of Rachel's supervision. But had Sharon genuinely believed Rachel's supervision to be inadequate, the issue arises of the demands students make of women academics and whether or not these demands are excessive. This is explored by Barnes-Powell and Letherby (1998:72). Focusing specifically on students wanting to discuss problems, they report that their students believed them to be:

> Always available ... students would present us with their problems in a variety of locations: walking between lectures; in the library; in the car park; in a café while at lunch; even in the toilet. ... Even on the rare occasions that [we] were able to get away for a half hour break, we would invariably return to our office to find queues of students enquiring where we had been because they had been trying to find us!

Barnes-Powell and Letherby describe students shouting and complaining when they 'failed' to be available. In a discussion of students shouting and screaming at academics, Letherby and Shiels (2001:129) note that while Letherby, a young woman academic, had encountered this, Shiels, a male academic with 25 years' service, had not. They identify it as a gendered experience. Perhaps women are easier to shout and scream at than men. Young women academics may be easier to mistreat. The way students make objections may involve verbal aggression or they may be of a more formal nature.

When Sharon was subsequently awarded a lower second, she made a formal appeal, citing Rachel's 'inadequate supervision'. Rachel was shocked by the complaint because: 'I'd kind of built up my reputation on the fact that I was a good teacher and my door was always open to my students. So it kind of ate at the heart of everything I thought I was good at.' Women respondents to Carson's (2001) study of student evaluations 'almost invariably characterised their personal teaching style, or women's teaching style in general, as pedagogically superior ... because of its informal and interactive qualities and their own conscientiousness' (p344). The way Rachel obtained a successful professional identity would seem to be consistent with that of many women academics.

However, whilst women academics can receive positive evaluations from students because of their approachability in the classroom and beyond, locating a substantial part of one's successful professional identity in approachability becomes problematic when a negative student evaluation is received. Moreover, one consequence of approachability is reduced time for career-enhancing research. Rachel said that when she saw Sharon's complaint, it 'absolutely made me question whether I was good at what I did at all or whether it was just luck that I had not been found out beforehand'. All academics are vulnerable to this way of responding to a student complaint – 'one of the striking features of academic life is that nearly everything is graded in more or less subtle ways' (Becher, 1989:56). Women are particularly susceptible to feeling undermined by a poor evaluation. Acker and Armenti (2004:20) observe that: 'as relative newcomers, [women] are subject ... to a felt need to prove themselves up to the task ...'. A participant in their studies of women academics commented at length about the stresses of academic life, saying: 'I think it is bad because you never feel good enough ... I constantly feel not good enough'. A young woman academic is even more susceptible to feelings of inadequacy because she has insufficient positive experiences to withstand a highly negative experience, such as a student complaint.

Rachel's colleagues and immediate – male – line manager were supportive, yet Rachel remained deeply distressed and self-doubting, particularly as Sharon was 'writing to various places ... using stronger and stronger language about me'. This should not be viewed as an unusual response indicating a teacher with a weak personality, which is what Rogers (2000) contended: when problems occur with students it is routine for academics to feel responsible. The example from Brown (2001) analysed at the start of this chapter is not unique. Hughes (2002: 100) says that one reason she finds student resistance to knowing about feminism disturbing is because 'student resistance represents a failure on my part to be an effective teacher. It suggests that *my endeavours* to find classroom practices that open up new spaces for knowing that will enthuse and create pleasure *are not proving to be successful*' (italics added).

Rachel gradually realised that Sharon's complaint was not what it seemed when she discovered that she was fabricating evidence: 'at that time I was almost thinking perhaps it was me [at fault], and then that changed. I didn't think it was me at all'. Rachel also discovered that: 'Sharon had a bit of a history of trying to manipulate tutors. She used to play people off against each other, to try and get her way'. Rachel started to think that 'it [the complaint] was about [wanting to do well] at all costs, whatever those costs may be'. She explained:

> [The project] was the biggest chunk of her third year. So if she could get this one boosted up, she probably saw it as having the biggest effect on her grade. It wouldn't have, actually, even if she had ended up with a first for her project she wouldn't have got a 2:i. A tutor she went to a couple of times after she had appealed sat her down and went through the calculations and showed her that even if she had ended up with a first for the project she wouldn't have been able to get a 2:i, but she was still determined.

Sharon's conduct as a finalist appears quite shrewd although ultimately ill-informed. As she wanted or needed a first class degree and might have been under significant pressure to achieve this, she may well have read the texts explaining how it's done. Race (1999:119), for instance, says that 'if you are expected to complete a dissertation in your final year, it is likely that it will contribute substantially towards the assessment profile of your degree. Excelling in your dissertation may have a strong bearing on ending up with a good degree'. Given that Rachel's feedback had implied that a first class dissertation mark was unlikely, Sharon might have investigated an alternative route to success. Evans and Gill (2001), in a practical text exploring the student-university relationship, note that a high proportion of student complaints concern poor or inadequate supervision. They advise that 'it cannot be overemphasised that it is important to raise any complaint about supervision ... in advance of taking the examination' (p64). So we can speculate that the evaluation of Rachel's supervision that Sharon made half way through the dissertation course may have been intended to lay the ground-work for later appeal if she needed it.

Rachel was not involved in most of the complaint proceedings. She said that: 'My Head of School saw it as for my own protection because I think he probably knew that I would take it personally, and at the time I kind of agreed, I thought, 'Wise people, they know what they are talking about''. This is a well-meaning management response but it is highly gendered. A young female academic is reduced to the status of a little girl, kept safely upstairs while daddy resolves a situation in which she is involved. Although Rachel said that at the time she was happy to trust the Head of School, 'I think, now, I would have liked to be more involved in refuting the accusations from the very beginning'. This demonstrates that an adult-to-adult response is needed from managers when unacceptable student conduct occurs, rather than a response which draws upon a discourse of parent and child.

Although Rachel referred to 'protection' from the Head of School, she questioned this reading of the male manager's response:

> The Head of School is a nice man [but] I got the impression that all of this was a hindrance and all of the whole situation could be done without and so although he said that he supported me fully and so did the department, I kind of got the impression that he would really rather that it had never come about in the first place. I kind of got the impression that he was outwardly being supportive but blamed me to a certain extent for the situation.

Although everyone would prefer that the complaint had not arisen, particularly as complaints are time-consuming and Rachel received support from managers, Rachel's feeling that she had been assigned blame is important, and resonates with cases explored in Chapter Four, where the attachment of blame to women academics is more blatant.

As Rachel was not involved in the appeal proceedings, she did not know whether the complaint had been resolved when the next academic year started. When the students returned, Rachel reflected deeply upon what had happened: 'I began to wonder is this a common event? Is this going to happen to me every four or five years? Do I need to put procedures in place to stop it happening again?'. Rachel decided that she must protect herself:

> I found myself distancing myself a lot from them [students] and trying to be protective of myself. It made a lot more work, making notes after every single meeting I had and trying to have witnesses as far as possible, spending hours over each email just in case I said something that could be misconstrued. ... [The procedures] were so time-consuming. I was working sixty hours a week anyway and at certain times it was impossible to keep up.

This process of 'watching your back' by recording words/actions is consistent with responses to Annandale's (1996) study of risk culture in nursing. Keeping records can be helpful if complaints arise later, and 'documentation is proliferating in the academy. Every transaction has to be specified and formalised' (Morley, 2003:132). Annandale makes the important point that nurses were never sure if 'they had covered themselves adequately ... because they can never totally predict which actions or aspects of a patient's care may be defined as a problem at a future date' (p439).

Rachel said that she felt 'very, very stressed and very, very depressed', despite having a successful year designing courses for a new single honours programme. She missed trusting her relationship with students and found the job and the procedures she had developed as self-protection exhausting. She found a suitable non-academic job and left the university. She told me: 'I think the only way is not to care, but I don't think there are many of us who can do that'.

The importance many women academics attach to caring for students (Cotterill and Waterhouse, 1998) suggests that women may be liable to respond as Rachel did to student complaints, especially if they suspect that managers are not entirely supportive. For women in the early years of their careers this susceptibility is heightened, as they have not as yet had the range of positive experiences of academia which could override a seriously negative experience such as a student complaint.

Discussion

Conventional wisdom in academia implies that the majority of the experiences analysed in this chapter are simply a consequence of the inexperience of the academics who encountered them: Eve did not respond effectively when the student shouted, so she felt under-mined by this experience. Alison did not make her non-favouritism clear to the women students, so they felt aggrieved. Rachel's super-vision skills were inadequately developed, resulting in a student complaint. Emily's lectures were so uninteresting that the student stopped attending and was annoyed when he was reprimanded. Conventional wisdom in academia implies that as these academic women become more experienced teachers, Eve will develop strate-gies for responding to disgruntled students, Alison's ways of indicat-ing non-favouritism will improve, Rachel will become a better supervisor and Emily a more interesting teacher.

My analyses challenge such conventional wisdom. New and ex-perienced academics can and usually do develop their teaching practice, so why it is uncritically assumed that any problems be-tween academic and student are due to teacher inadequacy? If academics pathologise teachers in this way, we absolve universities from having to recognise and respond to unacceptable student con-duct. What the interviewees encountered was unacceptable student conduct, not indications of their own inadequacy as teachers or supervisors.

Although their experiences would be unpleasant at any stage in an academic career, this chapter shows how unacceptable student con-duct can be particularly problematic for people beginning their academic careers. Eve's experiences demonstrate that mature stu-dents may not always show respect for a younger woman teacher and that an incident of unacceptable student conduct does not have to be conventionally 'serious' to cause significant damage at an early point in an academic career. If such incidents occur early in one's career and are not properly dealt with, the memory of them can be a hurdle to jump every time one enters a classroom. Alison's ex-periences demonstrate the relevance of supportive line manage-ment but equally indicate that young academics lack sufficient posi-tive experiences to weigh against the negative ones and so decide to leave the academy.

The range of student misconduct Emily encountered should start to raise awareness that unacceptable student conduct is not that rare. Emily started to distance herself from students because of the mis-conduct she encountered and the inadequate support from her line manager and co-workers. She reached this position early in her academic career and it may eventually make teaching and inter-acting with students so problematic that she may abandon this career. Rachel's account confirms this, showing how difficult it can be to distance oneself from students.

'The first years for new faculty are formative and lasting' (Boice, 1992:40). That is clear from this research. We see what has happened as Eve and Alison reach the end of their graduate teaching assistant-ship posts. Eve is now unsure whether she wants an academic career and Alison has definitely decided to take a break from academia. Early on in their careers as full-time permanent lecturers, Emily has become wary of students and is distancing herself from them, and Rachel has resigned with no intention of returning to academia. As Bagilhole (1994, quoted in Wilson, 2005:236) remarks: 'the most telling evidence of prejudice is most likely to be collected from the absentees, the women who have left the profession or who have been persuaded not to start in it'.

In their survey of stress encountered by UK academics, which revealed that 70 per cent of the 782 respondents found their jobs stressful and 44 per cent had seriously considered leaving academia in the last year, Kinman and Jones (2003) found that:

> The perception of an academic career as an ill-paid, stressful and demanding one will discourage many graduates from considering it. This, together with the fact that so many existing members of the workforce wish to leave the sector, has serious implications for the future of British higher education. (p36)

The analysis provided here of the salience of academic rank to risk of unacceptable student conduct should be extended to part-time faculty. In his study of the preparation and support of part-time teaching staff in twelve university departments, Nicol (2000) reports that departments were: 'concerned with how to deal with part-time teachers who proved to be unsatisfactory, for example in cases where they received poor feedback ratings from students. The natural course of action was sometimes to withdraw offers of further teaching' (p120). Rachel's experience shows that student dissatisfaction is not always objective and that even if student evaluation is well-intentioned they are not necessarily skilled evaluators. Emphasis upon student evaluations of the performance of teachers whom they may not respect as a consequence of academic rank is therefore questionable. The next chapter further explores student complaints.

3
Just don't say the f-word!

Josephine is a white, non-disabled, married, 33 year-old feminist academic with no children, employed at a post-1992 university. What she said in our interview shows how feminist identification can make an academic vulnerable to unacceptable student conduct and inappropriate managerial intervention in this era of new managerialism.

Although definitions of new managerialism are 'rather complex' (Deem, 1998:66), the term denotes a: 'move away from the traditional model of 'consensus' or administrative management towards a more assertive, 'executive' approach' (Davies and Thomas, 2001: 180) and involves increased accountability.

It is not just inexperience which can make academics vulnerable to the problems revealed in this book. Atwood (1994) notes that she encountered problems with students in her feminist classes when she was inexperienced *and* when she was experienced. This chapter does not claim to represent all feminists' experiences of unacceptable student conduct and managerial intervention, neither does it argue that these experiences are worse for feminist academics than for non-feminists. But it proposes that deploying the interpretation 'contrapower sexual harassment' (Benson, 1984) may subvert the new managerialist reading of staff-student problems as teacher inadequacy.

Feminism in the market-driven academy

In a discussion of the micro politics of the academy, Morley (1999: 173) analyses interviews with feminist academics and finds that

47

working in Women's Studies can be seen by colleagues as self-sabotage. One lecturer told her: 'I've been told by women academics, where I took this part-time job as a Women's Studies convenor, 'Oh what do you want to get yourself into that for? That's the death of your career'.'

In a study of campus violence in Canada, Osborne (1995:639) observes 'the existence of Women's Studies in universities exposes and challenges the andocentric, racist and heterosexist curriculum that has been typically characteristic of university teaching' and this has constructed feminist academics as threatening. Luke (1994 cited in Morley, 1999:160) remarks that 'women often find that once they publicly identify with a feminist politics, conservative male colleagues ignore or avoid them, and liberal colleagues consult or debate with them primarily on matters of gender'.

Letherby and Marchbank's (2001) survey of Women's Studies students reveals that students who enrol for Women's Studies degrees encounter problems too. They hear negative views, for instance that all Women's Studies students are lesbians who hate men. As Letherby and Marchbank (2001:589) tellingly remark: 'this is not to say that Women's Studies students do not hear positive things about Women's Studies, but they do not hear them very often'. Nevertheless, they stress that students enjoy Women's Studies modules in terms of content and teaching. Feminist academics also find classes stimulating. A senior lecturer in Morley's study commented:

> Oh the sheer pleasure of working with students, and feeling that you're all getting an enormous amount out of it. The feeling of warmth, the feeling of friendship and affection. The feeling that you're all in something together and actually making changes, achieving, doing things, the excitement, the pleasure in each other's work. (p164)

The Women's Studies classroom is not, however, always unproblematic for staff and students. This is apparent from Culley's (1985) analysis of teaching an introductory women's issues class. She explains:

> I need only mention to this group, for example, the readily available, publicly published statistics on education, employment categories, and income levels and we have begun. These facts are always met with a startling array of reactions: 'Who published those statistics?' (US Department of Labor). 'When was that?' (Any time before yesterday is pre-history). 'Those figures must be based on women who work part-time'. Or, 'A lot of women choose not to work, you

know – are they in there?'. Then, soon after, 'You can't get anywhere hating men, you can't blame them'. And quietly to themselves or to each other, 'I hear she's divorced, she's probably a lesbian or something'. (p212)

Culley thinks that: 'as painful as these efforts to distance, discount and deny may be to hear ... they must be allowed or the group will travel no farther' for 'only a full expression of these defensive responses will allow them to be examined, then to begin to fade, and to be transformed to anger acknowledged' and observes that 'anger is one important source of the energy for personal and social change in facilitating the transition from passivity to action' (p212).

This focus upon personal and social change is vital if we are to avoid a passively prejudiced society, but is it practical in contemporary higher education, where the market has become so significant? Consider Ritzer's (1996) views on 'McUniversity' and how recruitment and retention of students is vital because of the revenue students bring to universities. Many post-1992 universities in the UK are struggling to recruit students and are keen to retain them. So students need to be satisfied – and will they be satisfied if they experience anger in the classroom?

Higher education (HE) research demonstrates that many contemporary students do not want to be challenged by university study. Race (2001:20) observes on the subject of student motivation: 'there are students who simply don't seem to want to learn. There are students who don't seem to see why they may need to learn':

> Many young people are rebels. It's a natural enough stage of growing up. But this means that they aren't so keen to please us, and may be more willing to be sullen, uncooperative and passive. In our consumer-led society (and students are consumers) they are less likely to try to hide their dissatisfaction.

Whether or not students actually are consumers is questioned in Chapter Six. The point here is that the classification of people who show disrespect for academics and fellow students as 'rebels' is indulgent and unhelpful. 'Rebel' implies that the students are not responsible for their own actions and that it is academics who have to make adjustments. Is Race suggesting that academics are paid to keep students happy?

Race proposes that academics ask students what they think about a range of matters including their teachers. This seems to assume that students are always objective, and perfectly within their rights to behave disrespectfully. Chapter Two began to challenge these assumptions. As we focus here upon a feminist-identified woman teacher, we can learn from Messner's (2000) exploration of white guy habitus in a North American university classroom. He reports on junior faculty at his university, most of them women and/or people of colour, asking for a meeting with senior staff to discuss teaching:

> One of their main concerns was that they felt they were being judged negatively by students, especially when they taught emotionally charged and politically volatile courses such as social inequality or race and ethnic relations. Students, they stated, tended to ding them on course evaluations for 'lack of objectivity' in lectures and assigned readings. Furthermore, they observed that students did not always give them the respect that they believed they deserved. They were concerned with these patterns, both for pedagogical reasons and because they knew that student evaluations were part of the way that they were compared to their colleagues for merit ratings, promotions, and tenure decisions. Students' views of them were important, and they were consequential. (p457)

If the probability of problems for teachers of 'emotionally charged and politically volatile courses' (Messner, 2000:457) is juxtaposed with the infantilising of students, as exemplified by Race (2001), and the contemporary context of the student-as-consumer (Ritzer, 1996) accepted, it can be risky to explore feminist ideas in the university classroom. Messner makes it abundantly clear that problems in the feminist classroom are not necessarily the result of poor teaching. But this is not always recognised in HE, as we see in the case study of Josephine, where 'new managerialism, quality and the drive towards measurement and outcomes represents a new form of organisational masculinity for feminist educators to negotiate' (Morley, 2002:95).

Anti-feminism in the classroom

Josephine has been teaching full time at her current institution for three years, but had taught part time elsewhere when a doctoral student. She has successfully completed a programme of training for university teachers.

At the start of our interview, Josephine gave me photocopies of recent peer observation reports, saying: 'Last semester, a colleague watched my second year Women's Writing class. He said my teaching performance was 'excellent'. She gave me photocopies of student evaluation questionnaires where she was praised: 'Josephine is an excellent teacher. I've enjoyed this module very much' and 'I wish all my classes were like this one!' She was keen to stress the positive work relationship she enjoyed with most students, but told me she had recently encountered serious difficulties with a group of students.

The problems occurred just weeks after Josephine's teaching was pronounced 'excellent'. Approximately forty students (fifteen male) enrolled for her first year Gender and Media Studies module, a module which drew students from a range of degrees. Josephine adopted feminist pedagogy in this class, offering a 'challenge to the authoritarianism of traditional modes of pedagogy' (Morley, 2002:92). Note that although student-centred classes of this size might seem unwise, this was the practice of the department. Male academics seeking student involvement in first-year groups did not encounter problems with students. It is for 'others' that efforts to close the distance between students and teachers are problematic. Insisting upon formality risks creating an image of hierarchical distance and rigidity, whilst informality 'may contribute to a dynamic that infantilises and delegitimizes the professor's status in the classroom' (Messner, 2000:461). Josephine's experiences suggest that only teachers who are white, male, heterosexual, married, middle-class and non-disabled can safely apply feminist pedagogy.

Ten of the male students quickly became disenchanted with Josephine's module. In the first week, one repeatedly insisted, with increasing unpleasantness, that a point Josephine was making in a whole-group discussion was incorrect. Her point was supported by academic literature, which she had cited. Josephine wondered why this student had not just transferred to an alternative module immediately, given that he was so quickly dissatisfied. Not implausibly, she speculated retrospectively that he may have remained in order to cause trouble. Feminist pedagogy may be one reason for the student's dissatisfaction. Students often prefer teacher-led classes, but, as Morley (2002:92) asks, is this an 'example of reflexivity promoted by critical educators, or evidence of the extent to which dominant discourses of new managerialism speak us?' Even when students enjoy process-oriented feminist pedagogy, the privileging of the student voice it offers can be a heady prospect for students new to this approach to learning and teaching. What remains problematic is that a student believed that incivility was acceptable in the university classroom.

Jackson's study of women taking combined subjects degrees, including Women's Studies, at a post-1992 university is helpful. She explains that:

> when the students first embark upon their degrees and encounter different ways of being academic, they find it difficult to recognise or value alternative ways of learning, teaching and assessment. They often believe what they are told – that other subjects are more 'academic', and that women's studies is a 'soft' option for 'bolshy feminists'. It is not a real subject. (Jackson, 2000:293)

The male student's incivility in the first week of the Gender and Media Studies module might be a hysterical reaction to unfamiliar ways of learning and teaching. But more importantly, anti-feminism is evident. The prevalence and acceptability of anti-feminism in wider society means that feminism, feminist learning and teaching and the feminist teacher cannot be worthy of respect. Consequently male students find it easy to suspend the usual rules of interaction between students and teacher. Their conduct is not perceived as incivility: it is simply treating feminism, feminist learning and teaching, and a feminist academic with the contempt they rightly deserve. Indeed, aggressive questioning became a constant in the class. Josephine reported that:

> Perhaps the worst response, though, was saved for when we were discussing the way rape is presented in the media, with reference to feminist texts. I observed that all the women whose cases do not result in conviction cannot be lying. There was uproar: the ten male students were all shouting that women make malicious allegations. The noise was deafening and intimidating.

The male students clearly had personal opinions, but never drew upon academic literature to support their arguments. Once, a student insisted that an assigned reading 'just says all men are bastards'. Upon investigation, Josephine discovered that the men had not read it. She alerted them to a section of the reading which analysed men and masculinities in depth, and advised them to read it. This was received with derisive laughter and the men returned to idle chatter about last night's baseball game.

All the situations Josephine described are underpinned by sexism. The male students were effectively saying: 'we know better than you because we're men; we don't need to read books or think carefully because what we already know is better than your knowledge – your knowledge is premised upon man-hating'. As Messner (2000:459) explains, when he teaches gender studies he is

> ... automatically assumed to be very knowledgeable and fair-minded until I prove otherwise. It is the opposite for 'others' who are 'guilty until proven innocent'; and their 'guilt' is nearly impossible to

entirely overcome, given that they are likely to be teaching topics with which they have direct 'identity/connections' (e.g. women teaching gender, people of colour teaching race, etc).

I enquired how the rest of the group responded to this atmosphere of deep hostility towards Josephine and she replied:

> It was difficult to know. They were just how first years often are – unsure whether or not to give their opinions, waiting until they know more before they commit themselves in a whole class discussion. But when I put them into small groups to discuss topics they were certainly engaging with the course. As regards the problem with the minority of students, no one said anything when it was actually happening. My opinion was that they were far too intimidated. I felt intimidated, so I can understand why a first year wouldn't want to speak up. Much later, a few students were very supportive.

Luke's (1994) research into gendered differences in classroom inter-action finds that boys tend to out-talk girls by three to one. But here the male students were not just dominant in discussions: they had effectively taken control of the group, deciding what could and what could not be expressed, to the detriment of the women students and the woman teacher. It is not by chance that this happened in a feminist classroom: for as Luke argues: 'women who wish to critique the unifocal vision of masculine worldviews, the contradictions, omissions and misogynist fictions, find themselves quickly silenced...' (p216).

Josephine said she knew that action had to be taken: she was con-cerned for the majority of the group. Yet she did not seek the assis-tance of her line manager, the Head of the Humanities Department lest she be seen as an incompetent teacher: later, this concern was shown to be justified. She had questioned her own practice. She ex-plained:

> I had never experienced this [student misconduct] before, like this. Sure, there've been students who giggled at the back, who didn't read the set texts, wouldn't present material, whatever. There've been disagreements in class, too. But there's always been adult communication, and matters have been resolved. I've asked myself why this [situation] didn't seem to be the same. And I think that in comparison, this felt sinister from the start. It felt like they'd decided to attack me. I very quickly absolutely dreaded teaching the group, because it just felt that there would be no way to resolve the prob-lem.

Josephine made efforts to deal with the situation in a non-confrontational manner: she separated out the problematic male students, who had been sitting together:

> I said it was a good opportunity to get male and female views in all small group discussions, but then heckling wasn't just coming from one corner of the room, it was coming from everywhere.

She felt that: 'they'd decided to harass me, so physical separation wasn't a deterrent'. The fact that the men had decided to harass Josephine is one reason why any strategy to combat the problems in the class was futile. This may seem to indicate a conspiracy – and this interpretation is plausible in light of what happened next.

Not innocent until proven guilty, just guilty

The next week, the evening after teaching the Gender and Media Studies class, Josephine was called at home by her line manager to tell her she was the subject of a complaint. 'A group of male students had been to see the Dean of Faculty to say that I was disrespectful, unwilling to listen to their opinions. A bad teacher'. Josephine explained that students usually approach the course tutor, their year tutor or the Head of Department if they are unhappy with an aspect of their study programme but this time the students had headed straight for the top. The Dean of Faculty should have referred this back to the local level but he decided to intervene.

The Dean accepted the complaint against Josephine at once: she was not given an opportunity to respond to what she perceived to be a vexatious and malicious complaint underpinned by sexism towards a feminist woman academic. 'A decision was given to me by my line manager that I would be 'monitored' by a senior colleague. I must 'change my approach to students'. And I should remember that 'students pay our wages'.' The latter phrase is telling: the Dean of Faculty was effectively saying that students matter more than academic staff. Essentially, 'this university cannot afford to lose students, so even if students behave in a way you find unacceptable just put up with it, because if you don't then the institution will close and you'll be unemployed'. While the Dean's approach here may be perceived as the exercise of power: 'for the 'good' of the recipient [who probably wants to remain employed]' (Leathwood, 2000:166), underpinned by the requirements of quality assurance, this is nevertheless a context in which equal opportunities can be not just kept to a 'short agenda' – doing the minimum (Cockburn, 1991:216) – but can be entirely absent from the agenda.

Josephine explained to her line manager that she had felt victimised in the classroom by the group of men, eliciting the response that: 'whatever goes wrong in your classroom is your own fault'. This predictable statement draws upon a common-sense view that academics are expected to control the classroom. However, this is a highly simplistic understanding of the dynamics of power, expressed by a member of a profession which claims to value critical thinking. Josephine's line manager later threatened to have her disciplined by senior management if she continued to protest her innocence, reminding one of forced confessions in police states.

Later, Josephine discovered that she could take out a grievance against the Dean of Faculty but heard that a man who had done so had been dismissed. So she was trapped: she could either take out a grievance and risk dismissal for stepping out of line, or possibly lose her job anyway after being defined, and appearing to agree, that she was an incompetent teacher.

Josephine spent an anxious time considering this dilemma, wondering if she should contact her trade union or perhaps visit a solicitor. But she had not received any official letters about the students' complaint and the Dean of Faculty's response. Trade union and/or legal involvement might worsen the situation and, as Josephine noted, 'academic jobs are scarce'. Keeping one's academic career, whatever it takes, seems to be required of many academics. They have become docile, accommodating changes such as teaching quality audits and research assessment exercises with 'minimal resistance and opposition' (Morley, 199:30).

But Josephine absolutely refused to accept 'monitoring': 'I repeatedly stated, in heated meetings with my line manager, that the men were not 'just boisterous boys' (his words) but 'misogynists who are involved in a campaign against me'.' Josephine's line manager was annoyed by her deployment of feminist analysis to understand what had been going on, as revealed when he asked: 'Are you sure you're not just hiding behind feminist theory, when actually you've done something wrong?' Thus he was effectively saying that feminist insights should not be actively used to understand the social world. In Morley's words (1999:175), 'feminism is acceptable so long as it remains at a low level. Like little girls who are cutely allowed to be 'proper little madams', feminists are fine if they stay within the boundaries of acceptable feminine behaviour...'.

Third-year women students were shocked and appalled that a minority of first year students had behaved in an offensive way and had not been punished. The quiet women first year students found a voice too. Josephine reported that: 'They told me they deplored the situation. They recognised that I had been heckled in the classroom'. As we will see, the women's opinions counted for little in this macho-managed post-1992 university.

Consciousness-raising in the academy

The Dean of Faculty next instructed Josephine's line manager to re-solve the situation: the measures against Josephine must be imple-mented or he would ask the Director of Audit to inspect the depart-ment. A few hours later, whilst Josephine's line manager was con-sidering his response, the Dean of Faculty made the Director of Audit aware of the situation. Josephine's line manager was incensed by this, feeling that he was not being allowed to manage his own staff. Increasingly, he began to ally himself with Josephine rather than senior management: the situation became 'us and them' rather than 'you and us'.

Josephine took the opportunity to offer her line manager a feminist article exploring sexism in the classroom, which he reflected upon thoughtfully. He seemed to begin to see that sexism in the classroom was not necessarily a figment of Josephine's imagination but a fre-quent experience for women academics. He wrote a letter to the Dean of Faculty explaining that sexism had occurred in the class-room, and that senior management should not condone sexism. Josephine's line manager was prepared to admit that his initial res-ponse to the situation had been inappropriate. Thus one man who had understood little of feminist principles became a little more pro-feminist: consciousness was raised.

Josephine hoped that the situation was consciousness-raising also for the first year women students: young women, it is said, do not perceive gender inequality to be problematic in contemporary society. So if the first year women had any awareness of sexism they may have started to realise how women can be victimised in educa-tion and employment. As Culley (1985:213) remarks, 'the classroom itself can become ... a laboratory of what we have set out 'dis-passionately' to study'.

The customer must be satisfied ... especially if he's male

The Director of Audit said she had no intention of inspecting the department, and supported Josephine by insisting that 'staff development should never be punitive'. Josephine was relieved to

JUST DON'T SAY THE F-WORD!

encounter such support: perhaps it was not coincidental that this came from a senior colleague who is female.

Josephine doesn't know exactly what happened behind the scenes but at the time of our interview it appeared that the matter had been closed, as far as this is ever possible. Reflecting upon the experience, Josephine asked:

> How much dissatisfaction [from students] is too much? Actually, it seems that if *anyone* is dissatisfied, then they can make a complaint and you're in trouble – even if the rest of the group really enjoyed the course.

She felt that: 'it makes the job unbearable, even though it's the job I want'. She is right to be concerned about the implications of what happened. It has been proposed that lecturers should be promoted if they can demonstrate that their teaching is of high quality: in order to assess this it is suggested that the students be asked (see Furedi, 2001). This is consistent with HE in North America. Webber (2005: 186) writes that:

> As a junior tenure track faculty member [in Canada] I am acutely aware of the role of student evaluations and student complaints in the process of performance indicators (merit, tenure and promotion).

One of Webber's informants to a study of student resistance to feminism calls her teaching practices 'attempts to cultivate the Miss Congeniality prize'. Furedi picks this up, predicting that:

> Lecturers who know that their pay increments are closely linked to the approval that they receive from their students will learn to avoid teaching practices that might undermine their popularity. Many courses have already reduced or dropped theoretical themes and other 'difficult bits' from their programmes ... After all, customers are not there to be challenged.

The first student satisfaction survey took place in the UK in 2005: 170,000 final year students responded and statistics are now published via the Teaching Quality Information website: www.tqi.ac.uk. Student satisfaction is not yet linked to academic pay but if this happens there is potential for problems. The male students Josephine encountered, for instance, can be interpreted as customers who were 'not there to be challenged'. This market did not want a feminist woman teacher teaching a gender module. The women students would not have welcomed her dismissal but the Dean of Faculty's position seems to have been 'we need to keep the men happy'. Was this because it was the men who complained? People who complain are important: they expect redress. Disturbingly, the Dearing Report (The National Committee of Inquiry into Higher Education, 1997) notes an anticipated rise in student complaints, precipitated by the payment of fees. What if complaints are informed by prejudice and this is not acknowledged? Josephine's case shows how malicious and vexatious complaints may be accepted in the pursuit of student retention. This is rather like saying 'we'll believe anything you say, just don't leave'. Consequently, white, middle-class, heterosexual, able-bodied men may be enabled to dominate the academy *completely.*

If we intend to ensure the safety of feminist academics the place of feminism in the academy must be considered. Morley (2002:87) asks: 'whether forms of intervention aimed at personal and collective empowerment are naïve humanistic anachronisms in today's mass higher education system [where] the subject of higher education has been recast and reduced to the status of a potential worker, rather than a multi-dimensional citizen', and concludes that '... perhaps it is no longer feasible (if it ever was) to claim to empower others'. Eliminating feminism from higher education is not the answer: if feminist academics voluntarily withdraw from universities, male domination will go unchallenged. Instead, the aim should be to disrupt the current conceptualisation of unacceptable student conduct.

From 'resistance' to 'contrapower sexual harassment'

Many feminist educators who encounter problems with students highlight the concept of student 'resistance' in analyses of such experiences (e.g. Atwood, 1994; Moore, 1997; Titus, 2000; Webber, 2005). However well-meaning, this approach can be problematic. Atwood says that part of the problem of the student resistance she encountered related to her own impatience with the students and her inability to resolve conflicts in the classroom. She asserts that engaging in active listening and teaching students how to provide constructive feedback are helpful because 'students who feel heard are ... more likely to 'listen' to [and accept] other points of view from students, teachers and authors' (Atwood, 1994:138).

Of course, feminist teachers can seek to develop strategies to combat student resistance and of course feminists should remain optimistic that resistance can be overcome. But Atwood may lead us to believe, inappropriately, that feminist teachers *should* be able to develop strategies which will be successful in responding to student resistance. This would pathologise feminist teachers who encounter problems with students and be contrary to feminism, which is concerned with the empowerment – not disempowerment – of women.

Terms are needed which clarify the unacceptability of treating educators disrespectfully because without them, experiences like Josephine's remain unsayable and thus unactionable. This situation nurtures the claim that 'whatever goes wrong in your classroom is your own fault'.

Sexual harassment is a helpful concept. Wise and Stanley (1987:8) conceptualise sexual harassment as not just 'sexual' behaviour but 'any and all unwanted and intrusive behaviour of whatever kind which men force on women (or boys on girls, or men on girls, or boys on women)' (see Chapter One). This is consistent with Josephine's experiences of disrespect from men. We need to use the word 'contrapower' (Benson, 1984) to clarify how an academic was sexually harassed by her students.

'Contrapower' can be a controversial term when applied in HE. Grauerholz (1996:31) explains why this is so when she asks: 'is it really possible for a student – who possesses relatively little power – to sexually harass a faculty member who possesses considerable reward and expert power as well as legitimate authority?' Roiphe (1994), who objects to the sexual harassment discourse, argues that it is not:

> The mere fact of being a man doesn't give the male student so much power that he can plough through social hierarchies... The assumption that female students or faculty must be protected from the sexual harassment of male peers or inferiors promotes the regrettable idea that men are natively more powerful than women. Even if you argue, as many do, that in this society men are simply much more powerful than women, this is still a dangerous train of thought. It carries us someplace we don't want to be. Rules and laws based on the premise that all women need protection from all men, because they are so much weaker, serve only to reinforce the image of women as powerless. Our female professors ... are every bit as strong as their male counterparts. ... Female authority is not (and should not be seen as) so fragile that it shatters at the first sign of male sexuality. Any rules saying otherwise strip women, in the public eye, of their hard-earned authority.

This is an argument which actively seeks to deny the experiences of sexual harassment of particular groups of women: 'No, sorry, you can't have been sexually harassed. You're a lecturer and he's just a student'. Consequently, anything that goes wrong in your classroom has to be your own fault. We saw similar approaches relating to healthcare and education in Chapter One.

North American research demonstrating the prevalence of contra-power sexual harassment in universities shows how many academic women's experiences would be discounted if Roiphe's (1994) arguments were accepted. Grauerholz conducted a survey at a large public research institution in the US: 208 questionnaires were completed by women faculty members. Nearly half (47.6%) said they had experienced unwanted sexual conduct from students. Most common were sexist comments from students (32%). Other common experiences included undue attention (18%), obscene telephone calls (17%), verbal sexual comments (15%), body language (12%) and written sexual comments (8%). Two per cent of professors had experienced physical contact and one professor had been sexually assaulted by a student (Grauerholz, 1996). Eighty-two per cent of the incidents reported were perpetrated by men. Grauerholz states that: 'many women professors feel harassed by their male students [and this] reflects cultural power differences between men and women, and highlights the importance of gender in defining a woman's vulnerability to sexual harassment' (p797). Grauerholz's research is all the more significant because of the numbers involved. As contra-power sexual harassment has not yet been the main subject of any published research on sexual harassment in the UK, academic women's experiences of contrapower sexual harassment are not yet treated seriously – as Josephine discovered.

Discussion

HE is now often perceived as:

> A product one buys, rather than a process one enters ... Students are no longer constructed as recipients of a welfare service, but consumers of an expensive product, with ensuing rights, responsibilities and entitlements. ... this recasting has profoundly influenced both social relations and pedagogical processes in higher education. (Morley, 2002:86)

This chapter described a case of disrespect for a feminist academic at a post-1992 university by anti-feminist male students, their malicious accusations and the uncritical acceptance of their complaint by the male Dean of Faculty to keep these students/consumers happy. A feminist woman teaching challenging topics to students who have no wish to be challenged is not what is required for customer satisfaction ... and the customer must be satisfied.

At the same time, conventional wisdom in academia has it that if feminist academics encounter problems in the classroom it is because they are insufficiently skilled at teaching 'sensitive' topics such as gender studies: an interpretation easily extended to any sensitive topic, such as race and ethnicity, sexuality or religion. Educators can even collude: Bhopal states that when she teaches race and gender to women students, she tells them the classroom will be 'a forum in which students [will] be able to discuss issues around race in a safe, supportive and understanding environment' (Bhopal, 2002:113). She neither realises nor admits that this 'safe, supportive and understanding environment' may be impossible because of student responses to the teacher.

Case study and analysis in this chapter differ from conventional wisdom in academia, even that provided by arguably well-meaning feminist educators. Josephine's experiences revealed a classroom which was not safe. Rather than pathologising Josephine as an inadequate teacher or as unable to develop effective strategies with which to respond to student resistance or arguing against the f-word being used in the classroom, her experiences are identified as contrapower sexual harassment. Feminism has always been concerned with activism so feminists should be actively involved in a campaign against unacceptable student conduct, and contrapower sexual harassment may well be a valuable concept in this battle.

Understanding of the sexual harassment of academics by students is better developed in America. Chapter One discussed how concepts such as sexual harassment and bullying emerged and migrated to the UK. Now it is time for the UK to adopt the concept of contrapower sexual harassment. The starting point for analysis in this area should be the sympathetic research which has been considered in this chapter, not the victim-blaming approaches discussed in Chapter One, for Josephine's experiences have made clear that victim-blaming is currently a way in which managers intervene when academic women encounter unacceptable student conduct which can be conceptualised as contrapower sexual harassment.

The next chapter looks at how *any* academic woman, not just the new, relatively new or feminist, may encounter unacceptable student conduct and inappropriate managerial intervention.

4

Just girls who can't keep control?

This chapter moves beyond women graduate teaching assistants, women early career academics and feminist-identified academic women to explore how *any* woman in academia could be vulnerable to unacceptable student conduct and inappropriate managerial intervention. Two women provide information: Helen is a white, married, non-disabled, 35 year-old with no children who had been a Senior Lecturer in Sociology at a post-1992 university for eight years when she was stalked and physically attacked by a woman student. Stella is a white, single, non-disabled, 38 year-old with no children, who had experience in industry as well as university teaching when she joined a pre-1992 university to become a Senior Lecturer in Marketing, and was heckled by male students, one of whom physically attacked her in a lecture theatre.

The women in this chapter are in their mid to late 30s, which is hardly old. But is 'being older' differently defined and differently valued in different occupations (Maguire, 1996:27)? In academia the disadvantage of youth, as discussed in Chapter Two, is quickly replaced by the disadvantage of non-youth, for whilst academics in their 20s are often seen as too young for students to respect, women in their mid to late 30s are becoming old enough to be the mothers of 'traditional' students.

Quinn explores the importance of mothers for the 'traditional' and 'non-traditional' women students she interviewed. The women were 'drawn to bear witness on behalf of their mothers', yet felt 'a need to get away from them, even destroy them, to be able to think independently' (Quinn, 2004:377). So although 'mother' is not a fixed identity, mother concepts can be contradictory for students and cause problems when 'woman academic' and 'mother' become conflated. The theory of sex-role spill-over (Gutek and Morasch, 1982) indicates that gender roles such as 'mother' are often expected of women in their work roles: the woman academic may be perceived as an academic-woman-as-mother, regardless of whether she is indeed a mother.

The identity of academic-woman-as-mother is mediated by factors such as race, disability, sexuality, class, age and religion. For instance, Black women experience a particular conflation of the identities of 'mother' and 'woman academic'. King (1995:19) deplores the mythology of an 'ever-nurturing Black female presence such as that depicted by the racial historical images of the 'mammy''. If Black women embrace this role, it 'creates treacherous cycles of overextension and role overload' and if it is not embraced, it can create student 'rage and bewilderment' (King, 1995:19).

This chapter argues that Helen's and Stella's experiences of unacceptable student conduct and the inappropriate managerial interventions that followed are informed by stereotypical discourses of mothering. Good mothering is often conceptualised as requiring women to be nurturing and uncomplaining, whatever happens. We will see how Helen and Stella were accused by their male managers of just being 'girls who were not able to manage students' when they encountered student misconduct: essentially, they were perceived as having been unable to fulfil the requirements of mothering and thus as failing to achieve a suitably 'adult' identity. Consequently they were unsupported by managers. We also see that mother identification affects younger women, too. Mother-identification can be a powerful tactic managers use to pathologise women who are old enough to be the mothers of at least some of the students who are presenting difficulties.

An exploration of sexism in the academy at the end of the chapter draws together the threads of Chapters Two to Four to stress that the experiences described are firmly located in gender relations in higher education today.

Helen: '[The Head of Department] said: 'Right! Leave it with me!' ... A few days later I heard that he wasn't going to do anything, because he felt that Megan and I couldn't handle her...'

Helen related that she found Sally, a Sociology and Politics student, banging her head against the wall outside a seminar room. Sally confided in Helen that she had attempted suicide the previous night. 'I put her in touch with our counselling service and as a result of that she decided that she wanted to leave university'.

However, Sally did not withdraw. Three weeks later she returned to classes and started to approach Helen for support. Although universities have support services, 'increasing numbers of students wish to receive support not from the professional counsellors but from their course tutor (or equivalent) – someone they perceive as 'belonging' to them' (Marchbank and Letherby, 2002:144). As Helen was the person in whom Sally had confided the sensitive information that she had attempted suicide, it is understandable that she felt drawn back to her.

It may not be coincidental that this happened in a subject (Sociology) that draws upon personal experiences. As Cummins (2005:228) points out, 'in these courses, many of the subjects cause issues to bubble up and they evoke anguish, pain, unrealised hopes and dreams on behalf of the student-learner'. So while academics are often prepared to listen, they can become over-burdened with student problems. Helen initially felt sympathy for Sally but the student's demands soon moved beyond what Helen felt comfortable to offer:

> For about the next four months ... Sally was following me around, she was everywhere I went, the phone on my desk would constantly ring, she'd be ringing from the phone in the next hallway. ... She would ask me to meet her in town at the weekend and ask questions about where I lived. And then she would start to talk to me about her sexual relationships ... Obviously you do everything you can to discourage this, you don't meet, you don't give the information out, you find yourself in the end being quite brusque. (Cummins, 2005: 228)

Then Sally was allocated to Helen for project supervision. Meeting with Sally individually, Helen recalled, 'just became a complete nightmare. Suicide attempts constantly, wanting to tell me about that, details about sexual experiences ... it became really disturbing'. Helen's unease deepened still further after Sally was suspected of plagiarism in a sociology essay written for Helen's colleague and close friend, Megan. This was when Sally discovered Helen's ex-directory home telephone number. One night she rang Helen and admitted to the plagiarism and said that if action was taken against her, 'she knew that Megan parked her car in the badly-lit car park behind the Business Studies building and often worked late at night. She would be waiting for her in that car park'. Helen informed Megan about this threat and she herself started feeling threatened when she worked late at night, teaching an evening class in an isolated temporary classroom. Sally would stand behind the door, waiting for her. 'That was the only way I could get home. A couple of times I had to ring security and say 'can you come and escort me to the car?', and of course then they would come. But that didn't put her off. She would still come again'.

Helen and Megan decided it was time to raise the problems they were encountering formally in a staff meeting. They did not take the view held by many healthcare professionals: that since the person appeared so emotionally distressed, she was not responsible for her actions, and thus 'the primary responsibility for stopping it [the inappropriate conduct] lies with the health professional [or, in this instance, academic]' (Schneider *et al*, 1999:179). Instead, they expected their line manager to offer support for a situation which had begun as a need to care for a student but had developed into an increasingly threatening situation.

At the staff meeting, which Megan could not attend, Helen explained what had been happening. The male Head of Department said: 'Right! Leave it with me!'. Helen regarded this as positive, but 'a few days after that, I heard that he wasn't going to do anything, because he felt that Megan and I couldn't handle her'. So although the two women did not share his view, their manager's response was consistent with worst practice in healthcare settings (Hellzen *et al*, 2004): the discourse that front-line professionals should be able to cope with problematic individuals. And it indicates fear, ignorance or inexperience of mental health conditions from a manager who does not operate at the front-line.

The Head of Department's response also reveals the way in which women academics are perceived in university departments: that they are expected to be carers and should easily be able to respond to a troubled student. As Wheeler and Birtle (1993:160) relate about personal tutoring: 'there is a widely held belief that this type of work [pastoral care] is better done by women. Comments such as ... 'it is the sort of thing that comes naturally to women' are often heard'.

This draws upon 'female attributes such as nurturance, caring and empathy' (Carson, 2001:343), which Chan's (2004) study of teachers in Hong Kong shows are not qualities with which women are simply 'naturally endowed' but that rather they learn how to regulate their own emotions to secure the well-being of their charges.

There are certainly male academics who provide pastoral care to students. Yet as Letherby and Shiels (2001:128) remark, 'when men are responsive to students, it is often seen as additional to their responsibilities and as more of a gift, whereas when women provide it, it is seen as a natural aspect of their femininity and part of their jobs'. Wheeler and Birtle (1993:161) note 'an underlying assumption that men [academics] have got more important things to do with their time'. Men and women managers definitely should not need to become involved in the messy business of pastoral care. As Cotterill and Waterhouse (1998:13) explain:

> Managerial tasks and research count more highly than pastoral care. Viewed as rational, unemotional enterprises, they are allied with a 'masculinised' model of task accomplishment and completion, the quality of which can be scrutinised, policed and quantified. Care remains, as it always had been, qualitative, process oriented, ongoing and unmeasurable.

That women staff encounter difficulties in pastoral care and seek the assistance of managers seems to be viewed as inappropriate by this Head of Department, who appears to think he should be occupied with more important 'masculine' pursuits. He seems embarrassed that Helen has asked for his assistance – he not only refused to intervene in this student matter but could not tell his women staff what he decided. As one woman academic in another study remarked: 'The main quality I think that women are expected to bring to academia is the ability to care for and nurture students as if they were their own children, and to deal with the emotional messes and to clear up after things' (Wilson, 2005:241). Thus it appears from the man's perspective that Helen and Megan were being conceptualised as not just unable to cope with a problem but, more importantly and potentially more embarrassingly, as having failed to embrace the suitably adult identity of 'mother' required of women in HE. The discourse of blaming women as failed mothers eclipsed the discourse of stalking, which should have been dominant. This is unsurprising, for as Leonard (2001:223) observes: 'anecdotally it appears that universities are much more prepared to support men [who are the victims of stalking], for example in getting injunctions against women, than *vice versa*'.

Helen and Megan are not mothers but, as Cummins asserts, women academics are automatically burdened with 'compulsory mother-work', so they are contributing to 'mommy tracking' which, according to Williams (2000 quoted in Cummins, 2005:222) involves 'women who choose to put in fewer hours and spend more time with their families ... [and] are considered less serious by male colleagues'. And 'part of the traditional construct of mothering is to have no boundaries, needs and limits. Allowing oneself to be used up is a prerequisite of maternal care' (Morley, 2003:134).

The time at which Helen and Megan are being 'used up' is significant. As Helen reported: 'at the moment an awful lot of money is going into research profiles ... almost daily emails from different departments about monies that are available': 'we've been told we've got a year to get something published, or lose our jobs basically...'. This is clearly indicative of the emphasis in contemporary higher education upon activities which can be measured, such as publications, rather than caring, which cannot (Cotterill and Waterhouse, 1998). The research assessment exercise (RAE), which is the way in which research is assessed in the UK and used to allocate funding to institutions, puts pressure on staff to be research active. But Helen and Megan were not inviting the caring role in which they had been positioned so far. They were requesting help from their male manager and because it was not forthcoming they would be disadvantaged in their career progression. Morley (2003:23) notes, for instance, that those defined as research 'inactives' 'individually and collectively acquire the status of pariahs in higher education'.

The stereotypical understandings of women academics exemplified by the Head of Department also meant that Helen's and Megan's emotional and physical safety could be disregarded. The folly of the manager's position was demonstrated when Sally physically attacked Helen shortly after the staff meeting described. Helen went to teach a class and found Sally waiting outside the seminar room. As Sally had not recently attended supervisions, Helen asked her how her project was progressing. When Sally admitted that progress was slow, Helen said:

> 'Time really is getting on now, you must make a point to come and see me and see if we can turn this around' and the arms just went up and she just went and punched me on the shoulder. She made a physical threat but I can't remember the wording. It was something about a knife, was it a knife between my ribs or my shoulder blades? But she was hysterically screaming at me at this point.

Helen was concerned for the safety of the rest of the students she could see were approaching across the courtyard below, so she took Sally to the university nurse, leaving her in reception while she spoke to the nurse privately. After Helen outlined what had happened, the nurse said she already knew Sally. Helen took the opportunity to ask: 'can you just tell me, is she just a threat to herself or is she a threat to us?' and the nurse replied: 'Sally is clearly a threat to you. What she needs is a period of short term residential psychiatric care'.

The university should have been taking action, as a matter of health and safety, to protect Sally, fellow students and members of staff. This was not happening and, increasingly distressed, Sally was considering leaving the university with a Diploma of Higher Education rather than the degree for which she had enrolled. Helen, too, was thinking of leaving: 'I enrolled in a part-time accountancy course. I have stopped doing it now. It was a mad decision. I was far too busy. I just felt like I couldn't be in this any more, I couldn't do this any more'. Eventually Sally did depart with a Diploma of Higher Education.

But for Helen the experience did not end there. She still feels distressed by the responses she received: 'It wasn't taken seriously, you feel de-skilled, you feel hurt. ... I've made a conscious decision that if something like this happens again, I will not discuss it with people'. Interestingly, although probation officers who encounter violence from clients often want support, 'they may not record it [the violent incident] or talk to the senior fully in terms of there being a particular incident because they might feel as though in some way they're going to be blamed for it' (O'Beirne *et al*, 2003:184). Helen has now learned from personal experience that victim-blaming can happen if academics raise their concerns about interactions with students. Thus her decision not to mention such an issue again is understandable, but it means that what Helen has encountered remains individualised.

Helen and Megan should not have been held responsible by managers for the difficulties they encountered with Sally. There is no reason why women academics should be expected to be carers. Carson says that only two of her 31 respondents were happy to be seen as sympathetic counsellors, although the academic women respondents in her study often spoke positively about their nurturing qualities:

> There was considerable evidence of ambivalence or resentment. Some women staff described how pressured they felt by students'

and male colleagues' expectations into playing a part whose negative consequences, in terms of the personal time and emotional costs involved in dealing with demanding and sometimes distressed students, were considerable. (Carson, 2001:343)

This said, I do not believe that Helen's account is a story of women unable or unwilling to cope with a troubled student – even though that is how the male Head of Department chose to read it. Instead, the evidence suggests that Sally was encountering 'psychological disturbance', a term used to cover problems including 'psychiatric illness, behavioural disturbance and psychological and social difficulties, which may seriously and adversely affect the ability of students with such problems to pursue their studies adequately' (Association for University and College Counselling, 1999:1). A focus upon supporting Sally's mental health would have been more appropriate than classifying Helen and Megan as failed academic-women-as-mothers. This point is taken up in Chapter Six.

Stella: 'I was just a girl who wasn't able to manage the students'

When Stella started a new job as a Senior Lecturer in Marketing, she found a department male dominated by students as well as staff. The difficulties started immediately Stella went to teach an introductory module for students drawn from a range of disciplines. She described how at the first lecture:

> Students started to heckle. They were challenging my right to teach them. I was a woman, they were shouting. They were ill-behaved. They were very rude. This started to grow, so I took them aside in the break and said I wasn't tolerating this behaviour – the normal things that you would kind of expect to do as a senior lecturer.

Stella clearly felt that, as a senior lecturer, she could say what should not happen in a university classroom. But she did not realise why the men were heckling, that they did not want to be instructed by a woman and were treating Stella as a woman rather than as a senior lecturer qualified to teach her subject. The students behaved like unruly children, expecting Stella to be uncomplaining in the face of their disrespect and disruption. We can see that the mother discourse, clearly identifiable in Helen's case, is relevant even when not apparent in the way most commonly recognised in HE, when students and managers seemingly want academic women to respond in a motherly fashion to their personal problems.

Stella went to see the personal tutor of the worst behaved students and asked for them to be spoken to. 'I asked for their behaviour to be modified or I would eject them from the class'. 'They [the worst behaved students] bounced up to my office and demanded to know why I had reported them and there was quite a lot of aggression there'. The men were surprised and annoyed that Stella had taken action. This is typical. Letherby and Shiels (2001:127) report a male student calling a woman lecturer 'that mad woman' when she challenged his disruptive conduct. Similarly, academic women told Carson that: 'any tendency to be 'firm' or speak negatively to latecomers or chatterers is regarded as 'bossy' or 'schoolmarmish' and attracts some very rude comments from male students' (Carson, 2001:342). Robinson, writing about school-teaching, provides a relevant quote from a male teacher: he remarks that women teachers have difficulty with discipline because they 'tend to nag like mum' (Robinson, 2000:79). Clearly, many male students are unwilling to accept discipline from a woman academic. The academic woman-as-mother is not expected to be assertive, regardless of how the students behave. It is unsurprising, therefore, that after Stella complained to the men's personal tutor, the heckling in class worsened.

Later in the semester, the men's treatment of Stella reached a crescendo. During a break in a session, Stella returned a set of marked coursework to the group. The class was taking place in a tiered lecture theatre. Stella described what happened:

> Mark, one of the students I had reported, ran from the top of the room down to the front of the room and started waving his assignment in my face and was really aggressive and said that I had taken it out on him because he had behaved badly in class and that now he had failed his assignment and he wasn't having it.

Respondents to Carson's (2001) study also report that male students question the marks women academics award. Stella responded professionally to this aggressive challenging which suggested he felt 'entitled' to pass the assignment. Morley (2003:141) characterises the current 'entitlement culture' in HE as students being more concerned with 'what can I get?' rather than 'what should I do?'). Stella said she would speak to Mark later, and asked him to return to his seat.

> So he went back up to the top of the room, but ran back down a few minutes later because he was just incensed and his face was blood red. The whole incident culminated in him actually knocking me over because he got so aggressive and angry about the situation.

Other students were there, but I was actually intimidated, I stood up and told him to sit down. I should have ejected him or gone and got the police or something, because it actually was an assault, I realise now, but I was concerned about the situation and not leaving the class and trying to teach the rest of it and it happened in the break and I was sort of confused about what I could do and what I needed to do.

After the class, Mark went to Stella's office, still acting aggressively. Stella refused to speak to him. She told the Head of Department what had happened and together they interviewed Mark the next day: 'He again was quite aggressive, but wasn't as bad with the male person there'. There are echoes here of children playing up for an at-home mother, and finally calming down when their father returns home from the office. The Head of Department said Mark could have the essay re-marked if he liked, but 'like investments, they can go up or down'. Mark declined the offer. Stella said she would willingly provide feedback on a draft of his next essay so he could improve his performance. This was highly professional, perhaps beyond the call of duty when an interview which should have been concerned with the man's violence was transformed into a discussion of essay grading. This interview made clear to Mark that aggressive conduct towards Stella would go unchallenged.

Stella asked Mark's personal tutor for advice about managing the situation now. The personal tutor sent all the students an email explaining that bad behaviour was unacceptable but: 'it was evident to the students that it was me at the back of that, and the situation got worse'. So she had again been seen by the students as responding inappropriately for a woman academic-as-mother, who should accept whatever happens.

Stella decided that she would have to think of alternative ways to combat the problems. She stepped up the pressure to produce work in class. She required the students to prepare and deliver presentations: 'so that they would be less likely to heckle and harass':

During the presentations, however, I was watching a group and one of the men dropped his trousers and stuck his backside up in the air. I turned round because there was some pandemonium going on and caught the backside going back into the trousers, but I couldn't say who it was because they were all moving and trying to cover it up. I stopped the class and told them really very strongly that I wasn't accepting this.

The bare backside is a clear signal that the men refuse to respect a woman teacher, particularly one who has registered disapproval of

their conduct rather than accepting it. Such an explicit act is consistent with attention-seeking from children who want their disrespect for mother to be noted. Stella spoke to the Head of Department, telling him she was not prepared to accept such exposure in
the classroom, but 'he said that nothing would be done because it
was down to me and I was just a girl who wasn't able to manage the
students'. For the second time in this chapter we see a woman
academic explicitly held responsible for the conduct of students.
The Head of Department's interpretation of Stella is made clear by
the word 'girl': she has failed to adopt the suitably 'adult' identity of
academic-woman-as-mother. Academic-women-as-mothers are
perceived as having to be able to calm the children down. When that
does not happen, the academic woman is simply as a 'girl'.

Victim-blaming persisted in what happened next. The students had
taken a mid-term examination for another course, the results of
which were to be delivered to the students by her colleague, during
Stella's class. In the meantime, Stella had to teach a session. The students heckled constantly, particularly when Stella had difficulties
with power point. Eventually,

> I said 'I am stopping the lesson and we will reconvene tomorrow
> morning at nine am. What I am going to do now is leave the room
> and go and get the lecturer to give you your exam results'. So I had
> started to leave the room and they were saying 'oh no we shouldn't
> behave like this, we didn't mean to stop you, blah de blah'. As I was
> going out I was quite frustrated so I got upset. I went and got this
> guy and he did go in and give the results but as the way of things,
> this information [that she had been distressed] was given to my
> boss.

The next day, Stella went to discuss what had happened with the
Head of Department but he refused to speak to her. 'He said: 'I've
already had an investigation of this' and I said 'but you haven't
spoken to me!', and he said 'no, I've found out all I need to know''. He
told her he had 'spoken to the students and they've told me that
they're cruel to each other every day but when they were cruel to
you, you collapsed'. This echoes Josephine's experience of being 'not
innocent until proven guilty, just guilty' when a minority of students
complained to the Dean of Faculty (see Chapter Three). Verkuyten's
(2002) research exploring how school students make teachers
accountable for students' disruptive classroom conduct helps explain how Stella's students were able to convince the Head of
Department of the veracity of their version of events. Verkuyten explains that students will draw upon notions of consensus to make a

teacher accountable. Here, everyone except Stella is prepared to accept cruelty, so Stella must be over-sensitive. If this incident is considered in relation to Stella's previously assertive approach to student misconduct, a woman academic can always be seen as behaving inappropriately in the face of unacceptable student conduct: if she asserts her right to be respected she is seen as not fulfilling the stereotype of uncomplaining mother and if she shows a more stereotypically feminine response of distress, she is dismissed as a hysterical female.

When Stella asked to discuss the event with her line manager she further demonstrated non-feminine behaviour, which he did not appreciate as he had expected that the matter was now closed. This resonates with Coulter's (1995) example of an adult educator whose Head of Department reviewed her teaching very critically but would not allow her to respond to each criticism. Instead he told her: 'what you should have said was that you were very sorry, that you were going to do your very best to get all this straightened up and that next week you would invite me back to the classroom and everything would be just fine' (p36). As Coulter observes, 'women teachers are expected to show the appropriate deference to male authority and conduct themselves in ways which please men' (p37).

The mooning incident was the culmination of many weeks of disruption to Stella's class. 'Keeping order was considered the teachers' responsibility by ... students, who defined it as part of their job ... and if they cannot do so they are [in a student's words] 'a dead loss". The tutor to whom the students make this assertion appears to agree with this view (Verkuyten, 2002:115) and Stella's manager had obviously not progressed beyond such simplistic conceptualisation. Stella reported that:

> A couple of days later I got an offensive email from the Head of Department saying that I obviously wasn't capable of standing in front of students and I would have to think about whether I was going to give any value to them in a classroom and perhaps should just focus on research where I couldn't get into any bother.

The Head of Department is clearly incensed by the problems Stella is encountering in the classroom. He deeply resents having to spend time speaking to Stella and 'investigating' problems. He is obliged to become involved in the menial work of the department: what happens in the classroom. To stop this happening, maybe Stella should concentrate upon research because if she was researching rather than teaching, this 'failed' academic-woman-as-mother would not be so visible to the Head of Department. His suggestion could be seen as a career-enhancing proposal, as research is valued more highly than teaching (Jackson, 2002) but we must remember that Stella was hired as a senior lecturer, so is the suggestion that she stop teaching hinting that she should not be employed? What we can see from this is that whilst adoption of mothering can write women off professionally as 'just mothers' and not fellow intellectuals, being perceived as unable to adopt the identity of academic-woman-as-mother can prompt writing the woman off when it can be assumed that gendered identities will be embraced uncritically.

Despite encountering heckling, stalking and physical attacks from students, Helen's and Stella's male managers sought to make them responsible for what had happened to them, insisting that they were 'just girls who were not able to manage students'. The study of women teachers in Hong Kong that revealed the widespread view that 'women were naturally endowed and could care without much effort' (Chan, 2004:14) indicates that managers may simply not expect caring to be troublesome for women academics.

In their analysis of workplace bullying by peers/superiors in higher education, Simpson and Cohen (2004:179), report that women respondents to their survey: 'were more likely than men to perceive certain kinds of behaviour as threatening or unwelcome', whereas men 'tended to see bullying within a wider organisational context or to label it as part of a particular management technique' (p179-180). This gender difference is problematic because, 'if ... women are more likely than men to approach their managers to report bullying, and if managers are likely to be male, then it may not be surprising that in the majority of (formally and informally) reported cases, no action is taken' (p180). These studies contribute to understanding Helen's and Stella's male managers' disinterest in what happened to them.

Not surprisingly, Stella felt that the unacceptable student conduct and the managerial responses she encountered were deeply damaging. 'It has made me unsure about me as a person and what I can offer. ... it's as if they gouged out a wound and they just keep poking and poking at it until, you know, I've had to get some counselling'. Since our interview, Stella has resigned and returned to work in industry.

Discussion

Being a woman academic is clearly problematic, even when she has progressed beyond the early years of her career and is not teaching 'controversial' topics. Even when women 'have all the advantages', they cannot 'negotiate [themselves] out of *being female*' (Stanko, 1996:56, italics in original).

The women whose accounts are analysed in this chapter are in their mid to late thirties. Hoel and Cooper's (2000) workplace bullying study found that young employees were particularly likely to encounter bullying, while studies in Norway have found that older employees are more likely to be the targets of bullying. This suggests that women and men can be bullied for being young and for being older. Research has not yet addressed 'the manner in which ageism affects women at *every* point throughout their (working) lives' (Maguire, 2001:228). This book offers a contribution to that project. In the context of academia, the disadvantage of youth is quickly replaced by the disadvantage of non-youth: young academics are disrespected because they are considered not to 'know what they're talking about yet', as Alison explained (see Chapter Two), whereas slightly more experienced women are mistreated as they shift more firmly into mother-identification by their students and managers.

This is not to say that younger women academics are not expected to mother students. Mothering is expected from all women academics, as is emphasised when we look back at the interviews discussed in Chapters Two and Three. As women academics age they are increasingly identified as mothers rather than in other, equally inappropriate, domestic or sexual roles such as older sisters, aunts or girlfriends. Students and managers increasingly expect them to indulge students uncomplainingly whatever they do and to be punished if they do not. The sense of entitlement already discussed can be even more heightened, demanding yet greater indulgence and uncomplaining acceptance from the women academics whom students interpret as grandmothers, because grandmothers are expected to be even more indulgent and uncomplaining than mothers.

In academic circles conventional wisdom would support the way in which Helen's and Stella's experiences were dealt with by their line managers in accordance with the view that despite their teaching experience, the women have failed as university teachers. This fits the model of teacher development described in Chapter Two, where at the final stage teachers: 'start to develop professional tutor/ learner relationships with their students without taking their behaviour too personally' (Sharpe, 2000:134). Harlow's otherwise instructive analysis of the effect of race on university teachers' experiences and emotion management in the North American college classroom is useful in underlining this point. Harlow interviewed 29 white and 29 African American faculty ranging in age from 30-65 (the average age being 44). Harlow (2003:361) reports that 'many of the Black professors learned to ignore identity cues from interactions with students that challenged their professional identity' – while they were aware of racism in the classroom, they were able to prevent it from debilitating them. If we apply Harlow's thinking to the way Stella and Helen became frightened by students, causing Helen to try to retrain for a career in accountancy and Stella to return to industry, it would suggest that Helen and Stella have allowed sexism to debilitate them.

Not all analyses of student mistreatment of women faculty are problematic, but few equal Grahame's consideration of the experiences of women of colour teaching race, class and gender in America. She notes that even when these topics are not those being taught, 'we [women of colour] are still suspect. We do not really belong in the university, the telltale signs being the looks of surprise on students' faces when we enter classrooms' (Grahame, 2004:55). Grahame reports that students have challenged her teaching style, choice of assignments and grading and that women of colour colleagues encountered physical and verbal attacks. Rather than uncritically accepting individual responsibility for these experiences, she says that 'I figured something else was going on here' (p61). Grahame presents a seldom heard argument which is absolutely vital in research in the area of student 'resistance' to non-white, non-male, non-heterosexual, non-middle-class faculty:

> Making sense of students' contestations of our presence in the university requires an understanding of the broader institutional context in which our experiences were embedded. Thus, the analysis must move beyond the confines of classroom experience to consider our relations with others within the university (for example, faculty and administration) and how these experiences are organised by broader relations of ruling. (p55).

I conclude with a brief review of sexism in the academy, in which I relate the second-class status of women that prevails in the academy to the experiences analysed in Chapters Two, Three and Four.

The second-class status of women in the academy

Knights and Richards (2003) report that in the pre-1992 universities, while only nine per cent of professors are women; women make up 27 per cent of senior lecturers and 57 per cent of lecturers. Only 19 per cent of Deans of Faculty are women, and just seven higher education institutions are headed by a woman Vice-Chancellor or Principal, only two of them in the pre-1992 sector. Even when women are in the same jobs as men, research shows that they are paid less. Jackson cites the Bett Report (1999) to state that the gap can amount to £8,000 a year, and notes that women are dispropor-tionately represented in teaching, when 'for many universities, research is the defining activity, enjoying a higher status than lectur-ing' (Jackson, 2002:26).

Maguire highlights ageism against older academic women seeking to enter the academy, telling how a woman in her late 40s was en-couraged to apply for an academic post, only to see a 'bright young thing' appointed... 'young 'n' bright [seeming to be in] binary oppo-sition to old and dull' (Maguire, 1996:33). Kitzinger (1994) reports upon the difficulties she encountered as a lesbian attempting to enter academia. She says that after making an unsuccessful applica-tion for an academic job, she heard that 'the head of department had flatly refused to consider an out researcher on gay and lesbian issues, saying 'it would make a laughing stock of the department" (p134).

Once entry to the academy has been gained, humiliations remain linked to aspects of women's identities. Thompson (1998) cites an example of a Black woman academic who gained access to the library before it opened. A librarian asked her how she had done so, and they went back to ask the security officer why the door was open. He said he had assumed she was the cleaner.

Iantaffi draws attention to the experiences of academic women with disabilities, asserting that "well-functioning' bodies are ... often seen as a prerequisite for academic endeavours' (Iantaffi, 1996:182) and that having a disability challenges a woman's academic authority. On the experiences of working-class academic women, Hey declares that 'joining the club' is: 'lived as a grief – a gain that is constantly spun from the recognition and experience of a loss of a previous home without the pleasure of feeling safe in the new location' (Hey, 2003:325).

This chapter has featured women who are not mothers, but academia is problematic for mothers too (Munn-Giddings, 1998).

Probert (2005) feels that the impact of the household is the most important way in which women's careers are undermined, drawing attention to the needs of older children and not just issues of maternity leave and childcare facilities. But whether they be mothers or not beyond the academy:

> Management structures and students' expectations are gendered such that they are more inclined to make demands on women academics that are of a nurturing nature, whereas their expectations of the men are often restricted to academic advice. (Knights and Richards, 2003: 222)

Stella's experiences demonstrate that women are expected to accept misbehaviour from students/children unquestioningly, keeping what happens in the classroom away from male managers/fathers, who should be occupied with more important matters. Helen's experiences show that women are expected effortlessly to provide pastoral care and keep this messy aspect of academia hidden from male managers/fathers, who should not need to intervene. As we saw, their resistance to these manifestations of mothering in the academy evoked great displeasure from their students and managers.

Gendered expectations of academic-women-as-mothers are present in the cases discussed throughout the book. The mature students who spread rumours about Alison seemed to expect a woman academic to nurture them and were aggrieved when they perceived that she was nurturing the academic talents of a male student instead. The student who shouted at Eve seemed to want placating by mother. The male student who attacked Emily, like the female student who attacked Stella, refused to accept discipline from the academic-woman-as-mother. Emily's experiences with the other male student draw attention to the girlfriend discourse. Rachel's woman supervisee, like Helen's student, needed constant mother-work; and Josephine was perceived as a bad mother when she refused to renounce the feminist approach her students/children disliked. Except for Alison's woman line manager, management responses to these women were inappropriate. They were unhelpful to the women academics and ultimately to the students. As Morley (1999:109) notes, mothering can 'reinforce dependency and powerlessness in students'. Women academics should be viewed by managers and students as professional employees, not as mothers.

This chapter affirms the earlier cases showing that pathologising individual women for encountering problems with students is wrong. The women discussed in this chapter are not 'just girls who cannot manage students' but the nature of HE today strongly conveys to staff and students that women in universities are valued less highly than men. And it is in this context that women academics encounter bad behaviour from students. The experiences analysed in this book must be read in the context of the women's second-class citizenship in the academy, otherwise we absolve universities from taking account of what is known about the structural nature of women's oppression in academia in their responses to women who encounter problems with students. It is crucial that 'problems with students' be interpreted as 'unacceptable'.

How then should we conceptualise unacceptable student conduct? Grauerholz (1996) discusses contrapower sexual harassment, referring to expectations of mothering. Once we recognise that women's experiences of unacceptable student conduct and the resulting managerial intervention need to be seen in light of the pervasive sexism in higher education, the term 'sexism' may become just as useful in drawing attention to the unacceptability of particular experiences as the term 'contrapower sexual harassment' (Lee, 2001). In the US, Matchen and DeSouza (2000) deploy 'contrapower gender harassment' to describe instances of unacceptable student conduct towards academics that are gendered yet not conventionally 'sexual'.

So far, this book has shown how women experience abuse by students and mistreatment by managers. What happens when men academics are the victims of unacceptable student conduct is explored in Chapter Five.

5

Men are victims too

This chapter considers the experiences of five male academics who encountered unacceptable student conduct and managerial intervention: Steve, a white married 46 year-old with three children, who is a Senior Lecturer in Business Studies at a post-1992 university; Sam, a white married 50 year-old with two children, who is a Senior Lecturer in Economics at a post-1992 university; Ben, a white single 45 year-old with no children, who is a Senior Lecturer in Social Work at a post-1992 university; Brian, a white married 50 year-old with one child, who is a Senior Lecturer in Health at a post-1992 university; and Edward, a white disabled 65 year-old, married and with two children, who is a Senior Lecturer in Biology/Warden of a Hall of Residence at a pre-1992 university.

Like Eve and Alison, Steve encountered difficulties with dissatisfied mature students; Sam, like Rachel and Emily, was newly-appointed when a student raised a concern regarding his expertise; Ben, like Emily, was perceived sexually by one student and physically threatened by another; Brian, like Josephine, was the subject of a complaint focusing upon learning and teaching; and Edward, like Helen and Stella, was faced with out-of-control students. The evidence presented in this chapter makes it clear that the sorts of problems revealed in this book are not 'just' to be interpreted as the preserve of women in academia, be they graduate teaching assistants, in their early careers or feminist-identified. Academic men are victims too, and endure similar experiences.

This is not to imply that academic men have fixed identities. As Kerfoot and Whitehead (2000:187) state: 'often in the day to day banalities of organisational life as elsewhere, displays and enactments of manliness and of 'being a man' will shift across historical periods, over the lifetime of individuals and in differing contexts'. And like the women, academic men's experiences will be mediated by factors such as race, disability, sexuality, class, religion and age.

The men whose accounts are analysed here are in their 40s to 60s; there are no younger men. Thus, while Maguire (2001) notes that older professional men often experience greater respect compared with professional women of similar age, this chapter shows that older male academics may not always avoid unacceptable student conduct and inappropriate managerial intervention, indeed, this may well be related to their positioning in the academy as older men.

Following Leathwood (2000), I explore ways in which familial stereo-types, such as fathering which, like mothering, is not a fixed con-cept, can encroach inappropriately into academic men's ex-periences of employment in HE. Father stereotypes become rele-vant, for example, when academic men are old enough to be the fathers of the students who behave badly towards them, whether these men are actually fathers or not. When academic men feel that they may be perceived as not measuring up, which will be analysed with reference to selected father stereotypes, they recognise the danger of 'feminisation'. A way to interpret 'feminisation' is to recog-nise how 'taking up different styles in the workplace may be under-stood in gender-specific ways and assigned gender attributes' (Hay-wood and Mac an Ghaill, 2003:27).

Analysis of academic men's experiences of oppression by students and managers is not an inexplicable foray into anti-feminism in a feminist book. The theory put forward in this chapter connects with New's (2001:729) assertion that 'sociologists of gender hardly ever discuss the possibility that men are oppressed on the same dimen-sion as women, i.e. in respect of gender relations'. New feels that: 'almost all of those who now describe men as oppressed are part of the anti-feminist backlash, who deny the oppression of women and even see women, especially feminists, as oppressors of men' (p729). My analysis aims to disrupt the conventional wisdom in academia, with its failure to envisage academic men as the victims of un-acceptable student conduct, or its simplistic view that if men en-counter such experiences, they cannot be 'real men' (Lee, 2000b). Moreover, the debate must be extended beyond a simple yet valuable recognition of academic men as victims. This chapter sup-ports Gillespie's (1996:163) view, when she writes about male rape, that we need to have: 'engagement with the similarities and differences in meaning and impact rape has on women and men, and how these are both a product and reproduction of gendered power relations'.

The chapter concludes by reflecting upon the empirical material explored in the previous four chapters, to determine how we might conceptualise unacceptable student conduct and subsequent managerial intervention as sexual harassment, sexism, bullying or violence at work, in order to start a campaign against the problems revealed in this book.

Steve: '... you are talking to a guy who has travelled all round the world, who has run his own businesses – so for an institution to end up with someone like me with their head in their hands, I think is a staggering indictment'

Steve told me he had been employed at a struggling post-1992 university for several years, when, in the summer before the events explored here: 'we [academic staff in the faculty] were all called into a room and told our jobs were under threat. We could be dismissed at any time'. Steve found this particularly distressing because:

> I'd been through a terrible time with my previous employer: a vicious, nasty redundancy process where I was under threat for two years, constantly ... complete anxiety. And then to be told quite bluntly, in this sort of way, it brought back all the worst impact. I was in a state of nervous exhaustion.

This way of reporting emotional distress: recognising it but firmly stressing the understandable reasons for it, characterised my interview with Steve – perhaps because I was a younger woman. As Goodey (1997:412) observes: 'hegemonic masculinity does not allow for full-blown displays of vulnerability in front of girls and women'. – but 'hegemonic masculinity teaches boys to be careful about expressing feelings of vulnerability' (p403). She found that consequently: 'boys admit to and yet not admit to feelings of vulnerability which they rapidly cover up behind them ...' (p412). Steve's style of reporting his experiences illustrates how men may acknowledge vulnerability while actively seeking to resist the feminisation they fear this may evoke.

The redundancy threat was because of poor student recruitment, so clearing (the process in the UK through which intending students who have not yet secured university places seek to obtain them just before the autumn term begins) was a time of acute stress that year. Steve said that at clearing, 'we [academic staff] were told by senior management that our courses had got to recruit thirty to be viable, otherwise we'd got problems'. He explained that: 'I ended up at the beginning of the year with ten students for one course ... so I was taking anybody off the streets'. However, recruitment targets were not met and Steve found himself required to take responsibility for more teaching: almost the whole of the Higher National Diploma (HND) in Business Studies. As we shall see, this put him in a vulnerable position.

When Steve met the HND students, he noted that 'there were a group of mature students, who had been made redundant in their thirties, each with their own personal chip on their shoulder' and also 'people who wouldn't get in anywhere else'. Steve reflected retrospectively: 'we could have managed, apart from the fact that the mature students, part of their personalities is to engage in nasty, aggressive behaviour in a confrontational manner ...'. As the semester progressed Steve found the demands of the mature students more and more problematic, particularly in the context of his significant teaching commitments. He related how:

> I was losing track of things because I was actually having to teach four days a week, in three hour slots. I was preparing all weekend and these students were chewing through the information and then wanting more and saying so.

The students clearly needed more resources for their learning. Steve agreed with this but not the way in which the students were making their demands. He said: 'what they are trying to do is to get what they need for the course, which is the kind of logical bit of it. The manner in which they are going about that is in a bullying manner'. There are echoes here of Eve's experiences (Chapter Two) – in both cases we see mature students entering university with particular expectations and then feeling aggrieved when they perceive that these expectations are not being met. Allen reports that in 2004 over a third of students who complained to the Office of the Independent Adjudicator, 'which provides a complaint scheme for students who have failed to get their complaints resolved internally' (Allen, 2005: 19), were over-40s querying their degree classifications. The mature students Steve encountered, unlike Eve's student, who was still employed in a professional role, had suffered redundancy and needed to move beyond this via a qualification they now hoped to obtain. Their frustration is understandable, but does not make 'nasty, aggressive behaviour' appropriate.

The mature students soon stopped complaining to Steve and started complaining to his line manager because they realised that Steve, a rank and file member of staff, cannot make resources appear (Steve had tried to secure more resources for the students without success). The line manager's response was unhelpful: 'in front of all the students, [my line manager] said, 'Steve, I've got to say that I think you are really rather disorganised and I think it's up to you to sort of pull yourself together and sort all this out'.

Steve recognised the pressures under which senior managers at the university were working: they, too, were threatened with redundancy: 'so, you know, I was dealing with people who, I'd be talking to them, but they were not on this planet anyway; they were exhausted'. But he felt that the incident in the classroom had undermined him with the students. He recalled that they were: 'starting to disrespect me, and bypass me and go to [my line manager] instead'. Steve's experiences from this point onwards can be interpreted with reference to the juxtaposition of sex and age. Now that he has been classified publicly by his line manager as 'really rather disorganised', the students, who are already aggrieved, feel justified in perceiving Steve as a rather ineffectual middle-aged man who cannot cope with his teaching responsibilities and who, importantly, cannot be a satisfactory provider of resources for learning. As Steve was responsible for almost all the learning and teaching the students were undertaking, he was in a significant position *vis-à-vis* these students, a position which can be likened to fathering.

The fact that Steve is encountering problems fulfilling the father role draws in a particular discourse of fatherhood: that of the 'deadbeat dad'. Henwood and Procter (2003:339) describe this discourse as 'a highly punitive stance towards those who, for whatever reason, cannot meet traditionally gendered standards of conduct for fatherhood and masculinity'. One standard they refer to is the requirement for fathers to be providers. New (2001:742) observes that men are expected to cope with overwork: 'the masculine ideology of strength and endurance encourages men to accept and even take pride in ...[the] destructive effects of overwork...'.

Steve was distressed by the way the students were responding to him, in the context of overwork and lack of resources. He said: 'I got really upset and I was classically found with my head in my hands before a lesson'. He quickly added: 'now, you are talking to a guy who has travelled all round the world, who has run his own businesses – so for an institution to end up with someone like me with their head in their hands, I think is a staggering indictment'. From his account, we can see that Steve felt that he was in danger of being feminised by being: 'found with my head in my hands before a lesson', as this is not the conduct that would be expected from a 'real man'. Walton *et al* conducted focus groups with male factory workers in the North of England, to discuss men and emotions. The interviewees considered how they would respond if alerted to a death in the family while they were at work, and agreed that: 'the expression of grief outside the 'home' context is ... unthinkable' (Walton *et al*, 2004:408). As they observe, quoting Seidler (1991): 'to experience emotions is human, to control their expression is masculine' (p413). Steve had shown emotion at work, yet in reporting this in the interview he organised his words to indicate that this display of emotion should not be perceived as unmanly: he underlined his masculine status by stressing that he was a man who had: 'travelled all round the world, who has run his own businesses'. Steve was making it clear just how appalling this situation must have been for such a 'manly' man to have been adversely affected. As Haywood and Mac an Ghaill note: when 'existing cultural resources for a gendered claim to power are no longer available', 'men exaggerate ... their claims to masculinity' (p39).

Steve was then sent to occupational health and some part-time teaching cover was arranged for his classes. He was still required to continue with one-to-one student tutorials, but: 'I was then rejected entirely by the students'. Steve considered that his ill-health was the reason for this. He said: 'I know that I've been seen in this slightly vulnerable state in front of them, probably with a trembling bottom lip'. Thus, Steve had appeared not only as a 'deadbeat dad' who was unable to provide for his 'children', but as a man who did not respond in a suitably 'masculine' way to the stress he was encountering.

Steve explained to me why he had reacted in this way. He said he had had post-traumatic stress disorder (PTSD) since being the victim of a physical attack in a city street. PTSD typically involves: 're-experiencing ... the trauma' and causes 'significant impairment in functioning in various spheres of the victims' lives' (Mikkelsen and Einarsen, 2002:88). Steve told me exactly what happened and it had obviously been very serious. Thus again, the interview involved Steve stressing his masculine status: he may have appeared in a 'vulnerable state' in front of students, prompted by his PTSD, but what had caused the PTSD was horrific and would have adversely affected anybody, including a 'real man': an identity which Steve claimed.

Steve was still encountering problems with the students at the time of the interview. Reflecting upon the current situation, as the interview drew to a close, Steve mused: 'Do I restrain myself from putting a fist in their face? ... You could easily find someone who was made of lesser stuff than me taking a baseball bat to these guys without any problem at all'. The interview ended with Steve clearly positioning himself as a 'real man', a man who could resort to violence but probably would not do so as he was made of 'stronger stuff'. There are parallels with Walton *et al's* (2004) research, in which men referred to 'being upset' at football matches. They said that they demonstrated their distress via anger: anger is socially acceptable for men whilst crying is not (p407). Steve has already explained how he was upset, but what he is doing here, at the end of the interview, is reorganising that upset into anger/aggression, ending the interview by demonstrating socially acceptable male conduct.

Sam: 'I attended [the] lectures ... and I noticed that these two women at the back were basically ignoring what was being said...'

Sam's account indicates that vulnerability is a factor for newly-appointed staff, even if they are male, fifty and experienced, rather than twenty-five, female and inexperienced (in contrast, therefore, with Chapter Two) and that this vulnerability remains gendered. Sam's problems started when his woman line manager asked him to run seminars for students outside the Economics department, in an aspect of the subject in which he had no experience. Sam decided to attend the lectures, given by a woman. At the first lecture Sam noticed that: 'two women at the back were basically ignoring what was being said.' He was not prepared to tolerate such conduct in his seminars: 'what I decided to do was [tell these women that] if you do that in my seminar groups, then I'll get a grip of the situation right from the word go ... which is what I did when the opportunity arose'.

Apparently, the students were shocked to have expectations made clear in this rather firm way: 'they just looked at me as though I'd stepped off another planet...' Men and particularly older men teachers are generally, compared with most women teachers, expected and permitted by students to dispense discipline (Robinson, 2000; Chan, 2004), which may explain why Sam's woman co-worker did not challenge the students' misbehaviour in the lecture. But academic men whose dominant status can be questioned by students, for instance because they are newly-appointed, are not in a secure position from which to demand the respect to which they, as older men, may have felt they were entitled. The newly-appointed academic man is not – yet – the 'head of the household'.

In the next week's seminar, Vicky, one of the students Sam had reprimanded, was playing with a mobile phone. Sam said: 'I presume that's switched off?' She said 'yes, just checking my numbers. Would you like my mobile number, Sam? All the boys want my mobile phone number'. Vicky's question can be taken as a response to Sam's recent assertions of 'head of household' discipline, which are not being well received. She can be said to be putting Sam in a role which she finds more appropriate: a sexualised role in which Sam is seen as her equal or inferior. Sam is being positioned with the 'boys' who all want her mobile phone number, and not the position he seeks, that of the disciplining male teacher.

Sam's immediate response to Vicky's question was: 'well, no, in a word, no, I don't. Of course I don't'. He was clear in his rejection. We saw in Chapter One that men teachers 'may feel objectified, embarrassed and confused [by sexual harassment or sexualisation], but by evoking masculinity they can retrieve their superior position in power relations' (Lahelma *et al*, 2000:468). Sam's experience is that whilst men teachers can evoke masculinity in response to sexualisation or sexual harassment, in contrast to women teachers, for whom evoking femininity is not a helpful option, not all men will want or be able to respond in this way. They may simply be shocked by what has happened. The vehemence Sam described in his rejection of the phone number showed that he was shocked by Vicky's offer. And the students saw he was shocked.

When I asked if he saw what happened as sexual harassment, Sam agreed that it could be seen in that way, but said that: 'from a personal viewpoint, I found it all quite trivial and really rather pointless'. Clearly, men do not always wish to deploy the discourse of sexual harassment. This non-use of the term sexual harassment is not necessarily problematic, although men do need to be offered more opportunities to develop understanding of gender relations. What is most important is that Sam contributed this incident to an interview exploring unacceptable student conduct, so underlining his displeasure. This matters more than applying a particular interpretation to an event (Lee, 2001).

Vicky asked Sam's woman co-worker if Sam was qualified to teach that aspect of Economics and was told that Sam was: 'a full-time member of staff in the Economics department'. Vicky made a complaint to the head of her own department (Philosophy) that Sam was not qualified to teach the seminars he was facilitating. Sam was called to his line manager's office. She was, he said, 'somewhere south of friendly and supportive':

'If I thought you were winging it' – she said, exact words as I recall – 'then you would be in trouble'. I said 'I have never ever winged a class in my life, nor do I intend to. I never ever give anything less than 100 per cent, but we must bear in mind the context I was in, teaching an area of which I have no knowledge'.

The situation was resolved and Sam encountered no further problems from Vicky. It might have been worse, as indicated by Fine's memoir of being stalked by a woman student, Mrs M. Fine relates how his experiences of stalking began after a problem arose at a seminar group: Mrs M was annoyed because one of her peers had not prepared for a presentation they were making together. Later, Fine met with Mrs M and 'advised her to focus on her own studies rather than the shortcomings of other students' (Fine, 1997:11). Afterwards, Mrs M alleged that Fine had sexually propositioned her during that meeting, and many years of stalking began. Certainly, as Fine (p2) notes, 'most stalkers are men and most victims of stalking are women' but personal identity is relevant to how people experience unacceptable student conduct: Fine notes the relevance of an aspect of his personal identity, separation from his female partner, to the problems he encountered: 'I felt the vulnerability of one who has lost his place in the world and was convinced it showed in my face, voice and gestures' (p146). There is a resonance here with Sam. As a newly-appointed member of staff, Sam had not yet secured his place in his university department as an older academic man who was entitled to dispense discipline to students.

The problems he encountered were set in progress by Sam's line manager's inappropriate placing of her new member of staff. When our interview took place a year later, Sam was clear that he would now feel able to refuse to teach material with which he was not familiar. Nevertheless, this should not be taken to imply that what happened to Sam was inconsequential. It was not merely an experience which could only take place at the start of a career in a new department and which would soon be forgotten. How academics are received in a new environment can have a significant effect upon how they respond to that environment for a long while afterwards. Sam certainly remained wary of his line manager after this incident. There are similarities between this case and the cases considered in Chapter Two.

Ben: 'When we were telling [the Dean] about this student and his threats, his response was 'well, I'd better see him for a chat before I speak with you again', this sort of nonsense...'

Ben was serving his notice when I met him. His most recent experiences of unacceptable student conduct and the managerial intervention had convinced him that he no longer wished to continue in his post of Senior Lecturer in Social Work, a post he had held for several years. He was returning to being a practitioner.

First, Ben recalled that Lucy, a married student in her 30s, had been: 'demanding attention, wanting to keep my focus on her and making sort of teasing type responses to things I was saying or doing'. She was behaving like the clingy student of Emily's (see Chapter Two). Ben was being perceived not as an academic but in an inappropriately domestic way, as a potential sexual partner. He saw this as 'sexual harassment', indicating that men do not always dismiss this discourse (Lee, 2000b; DeSouza, 2003). We should note the relevance of equality issues to Ben's disciplinary background, which has affected how he interprets experiences. As the problems persisted, Ben said that sessions were: 'imbued with quite a lot of anxiety' because he was aware of: 'how [that] can end for the people concerned, even though this attraction was in no way reciprocated'. Ben's woman line manager was supportive:

> She convened a meeting with Lucy and basically read the riot act to her, along the lines of: we are looking for an improvement in your behaviour generally but you are not going to be having any individual tutorials with Ben, you'll be with a female member of staff, you won't see Ben on his own. A fairly rigorous response, so I felt thoroughly underpinned.

This resolved the situation. At the interview Ben reflected upon what had happened from the position of having been supported and the problem resolved. He remarked that he had understood that 'it was almost like, coming on the course [Lucy] was sort of seeing vistas of a whole new world opening up for her in a lot of different aspects of her life...' so he felt sympathy for her. In contrast to women professionals who are sexually harassed by male non-staff (see Hellzen *et al*, 2004), Ben was not saying that he was physically frightened of his sexual harasser, but his fear of accusations of reciprocated sexual interest should not be underestimated. It is not clear that academic men encounter any significant sanctions, even if they are found to have sexually exploited students (Carter and Jeffs, 1995) but it is relevant to recall from Chapter One Dingwall's observation that 'it is what people take to be real that has real consequences'.

The current problem Ben was encountering involved a student, David, who was on placement. David made threats to the placement provider and later to Ben. The threat to Ben was particularly problematic as Ben was renting a house opposite David's flat. Ben needed to move house immediately. Ben and his line manager went to see the Dean to arrange for Ben to have a room in a hall of residence. Ben explained that:

> What I took away from the initial meeting with the Dean was that I would be looking at a month in the hall, at the faculty's expense, because I was still having to pay a month's rent to cover my rented house even though I wasn't in it.

Two weeks later the Dean indicated that Ben was: 'expecting to stay in halls indefinitely at the faculty's expense' and was therefore: 'trying to defraud the faculty'. Ben had already written to student accommodation asking for invoices to be sent to him. He wrote to student accommodation again, saying that the Dean was concerned: 'at which point [the Dean] blew a fuse. He must have hammered the email out. The spelling mistakes were all too apparent. And that was the start of a fairly long and unhappy relationship.' The Dean decided not to believe the social work staff's account of David's conduct towards the placement provider and Ben; David remained at the university. Ben explained that:

> What stands out in this is the Dean's contempt. That is not putting it too strongly. When we were telling him about this student and his threats, his response was 'well, I'd better see him for a chat before I speak with you again' – this sort of nonsense, this drivel. All amounting to contempt for our account and our welfare.

Ben referred to his experiences with David in a matter-of-fact way, simply describing what had happened. From Ben's account, however, it seemed that the Dean was not matter-of-fact: he was demonstrating distinct unease with, even fear of, the situation. The Dean's responses to Ben shows an expectation of how men are expected to behave, as previously seen in the examples of how men encounter bullying in the Civil Service (Lee, 2002a). The Dean's responses to Ben exemplify a view that a 'real man', a professional in his 40s, should not be frightened if threatened by another, younger, man in the 'subordinate' position of student; and that an older, male teacher should be able to effectively impose discipline (Chan, 2004; Robinson, 2000). Haywood and Mac an Ghaill's (2003:64) point that: 'an inability to be powerful and authoritative corresponds closely with a culturally ascribed inability to be a 'proper man" is relevant here. For Ben to move house as a result of the threat is seen as embarrassing, an indication of failed manhood: there are similarities between this situation and Helen's and Stella's experiences (see Chapter Four). As a consequence, Ben's conduct has to be reclassified as an attempt to 'defraud the faculty', an interpretation the Dean can cope with more readily. As Kerfoot and Whitehead (2000:192) note, 'management and the masculinities enacted therein combine in unending struggle to portray boldness and bravado and to hide fear and self-doubt'.

Choosing an accusation of fraud is important, too. This case reveals the worst excesses of new managerialism in the sense of demonstrating a tendency to place financial considerations before staff welfare. Ben remarked that a colleague had said that the Dean was noted for taking the side of students rather than staff but Ben made clear why he felt the Dean did this: 'I actually don't think he gives a fuck about students, all that gives him is convenient ammunition ... if there is something that he can use against his staff to demoralise and undermine he will do so'. As Johnson and Deem (2003:290) point out: 'Whilst UK higher education policy now heavily emphasises the student, our data, both at institutional and individual level ... focus on the organisational, resources and time implications of the student body, rather than the student him/herself'.

Brian: I thought what I was doing was good and sound. It was a sharp shock to recognise that people could perceive me in, not only negative, but hostile ways...

Brian told me he encountered problems with a small number of students who were taking one of his modules as part of a postgraduate course. His use of group work in this module shocked a number of the new postgraduates, who were more accustomed to making notes in lectures. One young woman student, Natalie, raised concerns with Brian. He explained that he valued 'the social construction of knowledge based on shared experience' and observed that: 'perhaps [this] was not the right module for her'.

Natalie stayed registered for the module but remained unconvinced by the learning and teaching methods employed. Several weeks later she complained to Brian again: 'we had, not a confrontation but an unhelpful discussion, where she repeated her observations that group work wasn't appropriate and she wanted a better way of gaining her degree'. This can be interpreted as a student desire to have academics transmit knowledge, rather than what Brian wanted to do, which was: 'provide [students] with a high powered, highly charged experience that they can go away and make some sense of within the context of the complexities of their working lives which, of course, they are coming to the university to enhance'. There are echoes here of Josephine's experiences of using feminist pedagogy (Chapter Three). Morley (2002:92) notes that in the current academic climate, many students reject 'process-oriented feminist pedagogy in favour of more tangible products such as teacher-led lectures'. So Natalie can be said to be interpreting Brian's approach as not 'giving' sufficiently for degrees and credentials to be obtained satisfactorily. Brian was well aware that group work can be perceived as a 'high-risk strategy' for the tutor. He observed that: 'you make yourself vulnerable to the charges that they don't get it, they don't understand, you've no expertise, you're lazy...'.

Whilst both men and women encounter such charges, it is likely that academic men more than women are expected by their students to transmit knowledge via lectures rather than to facilitate group work. The stereotype of the 'real academic man' is of a supremely self-con-fident individual strutting his stuff in a packed lecture theatre. Failing to adopt this stereotype can be taken by students as inability to teach in this way. A man facilitating group work may be perceived as 'not a real man', and thus feminised and rejected. The way Brian responded to students is also relevant. For while he may be said to have been providing a stereotypically 'non-masculine' learning ex-perience, he was not providing the stereotypically 'feminine' ap-proach to students – academic women are usually expected to mother students. Rachel, for instance (Chapter Two) said: 'my door was always open'. Brian's door was definitely not. He explained:

> I really like teaching. I don't particularly like students, you know, car-ing about them personally ... I'm really interested in their learning and I'm really interested in how they go about that. ... I don't parti-cularly want to become friends with them. I'm not unsociable and I'm not unapproachable, but I make a point of not caring too much about what they think about me and what I think about them ... There is nothing worse than the tutor who never leaves their stu-dents alone and goes to the bar and all that, because [the students] don't have the chance to sound off. ... if it's not making a difference and making you uncomfortable and unsure, what is it doing if it's all a warm coating? It's not actually taking people on.

This is a view of students that many academic men can safely take: in Chapter Four, I quote Letherby and Shiels (2001:128): 'when men are responsive to students, it is often seen as additional to their responsibilities and as more of a gift, whereas when women provide it, it is seen as a natural aspect of their femininity and part of their jobs'. This approach is rendered problematic by Brian's student-centred teaching. Students may expect a man, particularly an older man, who adopts student-centred teaching to be a 'new, attentive, caring or nurturing father' (Henwood and Procter, 2003:337). Instead, Brian's approach to students makes him appear to be rather detached, an individual who, if fathering is required (and inappropriate familial stereotypes do have a disappointing currency in higher education), appears to be providing a type of fathering perceived as unfashionable and unhelpful. So Brian appears not just to fail to be a 'real academic man' but fails also to be a 'nurturing father' to his students in the student-centred classes. Natalie went on to make a formal complaint. Brian reflected on how he felt when he was told:

> What I felt in my heart was that I thought what I was doing was good and sound. It was a sharp shock to recognise that people could perceive of me in not only negative, but hostile ways – so that was a cause for concern. It was like a physical assault. I mean, when I first received the letter from the Head of Health [telling him that there had been a complaint], I felt like I'd been hit really hard, I felt sick. There's no way I can ... actually it's chilling me now.

That Brian said he was distressed by the complaint could be interpreted as feminising. Men are certainly aware of the dangers of feminisation: for instance, Brian's likening of knowledge of the complaint to a 'physical assault ... like I'd been hit really hard' underlined the point that to be the subject of a complaint is not trivial. There is an echo of Goodey's (1997:412) point that 'boys admit to and yet not admit to feelings of vulnerability which they rapidly cover up behind them...'.

Brian's Head of Department took the view that the complaint was 'serious' and that they needed to 'make sure responses are full and founded'. Brian, however, like Josephine and Rachel was not kept informed of what was happening. He never saw the letter Natalie had written and was not even clear about the exact nature of the complaint. Brian found the situation very stressful:

> It felt very intimidating, really, to think that trouble was round the corner as a consequence of this. The fact that my Head of Depart-

94

ment had – I don't know whether he had to or felt he was obliged to – reported it on to the School Chair of Teaching Standards and the Head of School, was actually quite intimidating, given that these are powerful people. I had spent years on short term contracts, so you are vulnerable to a lot of people who are just being protective of the institution. You know, it looks as if you are rocking the quality boat. That isn't an attractive proposition.

Brian only told one woman colleague what was happening. He explained:

It [the complaint] made me feel very vulnerable, it didn't feel particularly this was something we could talk about and get assistance with. I don't know. It just spreads the version around that you are not as good as you think you are.

She advised that 'the safest thing to do in a university is to give a lecture, because even if you're bored at least you are conforming to the model'. Brian did indeed rethink his learning and teaching strategy for the second semester of the module because the complaint: 'really did sort of attack my confidence', and so:

What [the complaint] did for the remainder, well certainly the remainder of that academic year was make me feel the need to inject fairly substantial chunks of theory from time to time as well as continuing to do group work and I didn't think it was appropriate.

Thus, as a consequence of the complaint, students were given a more formulaic approach to teaching. Brian was encouraged when a male student who had previously been disgruntled and called the sessions 'a waste of time' returned to the class in the second semester. Brian reported: 'he said: 'it was only when I started to write the paper that I realised what it was that I was doing' and there was a sense around that that was the student experience'.

It was over a year later, many months after the complaint had been resolved, with no disciplinary consequences for Brian and after Natalie had withdrawn from the course, that Brian felt able to return cautiously to his previous learning and teaching methods. The complaint took away some of his enjoyment of teaching. There are similarities with what Josephine said: fear of student complaint, 'makes the job unbearable, even though it's the job I want'.

Edward: 'I have the power to throw [students] out of my hall, but the university doesn't like me doing that. They try to make it difficult for me'

When I met Edward, he was just retiring as warden of a hall of residence after twenty years. He wanted to tell me how a 'mafia organisation' of students and graduates had sought, over many years, to take control of the hall. This 'mafia organisation' played loud music late at night, super-glued doors, wired doors to mains electricity, dealt drugs, organised prostitution rackets and committed rapes. Edward brought a photograph of guns and knives he had confiscated from the students in the 'mafia organisation' to the interview. He told me:

> One of these knives was a flick knife, and I destroyed that immediately because they are totally illegal ... and that's just a sheath knife ... None of these were actually pulled on anyone. They are usually just found. Usually the cleaners say to me that 'so-and-so has got a gun', or that 'they are firing them in the rooms or in the halls' and that's what draws my attention to them. None of them have been used in a threatening manner, but you think how long before somebody does...?

Edward drew attention to how the 'mafia organisation' had attempted to intimidate tutors at the hall of residence over the years because: 'there is a certain amount of attempting to persuade staff to leave them completely alone, to their own devices so that they can get up to, you know...' He recalled that one male tutor: 'had just gone into the bar and he was trying to be friendly and just talk to them and they just grabbed him and chucked him in a cold bath'. A woman tutor was surrounded and threatened by a group of male students:

> And she just walloped the first guy and he went down. She hit him hard. She was big and tall and quite strong. He was trying to take action against her, and I said: 'I was there and I didn't see anything. I saw you threatening and intimidating her but I didn't see her hit you'.

Edward had also encountered problems with groups of students. He explained: 'they are usually drunk, of course, or on other things. I have been surrounded by packs at times who have been threatening late at night'. He explained that: 'none of them like to push it too far. Nobody has taken a swing at me for example, it's usually just verbal abuse'. Edward was clear that students 'pay heavily' for this because: 'I don't tolerate much at all, and they had better be very grovelling in their apology'. One male student had been physically threatening, pointing a billiard cue at Edward.

> I was younger then. I could take care of myself, and I could certainly have taken care of him, and when I warned him that if he didn't lower the cue, I was going to hurt him – I just said: 'if you don't put that cue down I'm going to do you serious injury' – I think he believed me, fortunately.

Thus Edward presented himself and most of the tutors who had remained in the hall as tough people responding to often out-of-control students. The way he characterised hall staff demonstrates similarities with studies of bouncers or door supervisors – which show this as a 'masculinity occupation that valorises violence, physicality and hardness' (Monaghan, 2004:462). The analogy remained pertinent when Edward related how the university responded to what happened in the hall, saying: 'the university continually ties my hands. I have the power to fine students, but the university doesn't like me doing that. I have the power to throw them out of my hall, but the university doesn't like me doing that. They try to make it difficult for me'. And in a 'market society geared towards profit maximisation', licensees want to keep customers, thus they: 'often treated door staff ... as disposable, replaceable bodies' (Monaghan, 2004:461). In this case, the university appears more concerned to retain problematic students than to protect unproblematic students and hall staff.

The university's approach can be interpreted not just in terms of financial considerations but as stereotyping the wardens/tutors as parents. Two conceptualisations of fathering are particularly relevant to Edward's experiences. The first is the traditional 'family values' approach with the man as head of the household, and the second is the discourse of the 'deadbeat dad': 'a highly punitive stance towards those who, for whatever reason, cannot meet traditionally gendered standards of conduct for fatherhood and masculinity' (Henwood and Procter, 2003:339). One important standard of conduct is the requirement for fathers to be effective disciplinarians. In a 'traditional' family, the children/students would not dare to defy their father – according to this model, senior management at the university would not need to involve themselves with what happens in the hall of residence. But when Edward wants to expel students from the hall of residence he is demonstrating to senior managers that he cannot keep order, so he becomes a deadbeat dad: an embarrassing failed father who has to seek help from beyond the immediate family. This echoes Helen's and Stella's experiences discussed in Chapter Four.

Edward stressed that he did not feel powerless when faced with the unruly students, as 'the average kind of middle-class student is sort of kiddies stuff to me'. Yet significantly, when I asked if he would talk about what happened in the hall with his fellow academics, he said he seldom did because of 'I suppose, fear of not being believed and fear of, I suppose, giving an impression that I couldn't handle it...'. As Haywood and Mac an Ghaill (2003:64) point out: 'an inability to be powerful and authoritative corresponds closely with a culturally ascribed inability to be a 'proper man''. Edward is aware that mis-behaviour in the hall, even though he sees it as beyond what anyone could resolve, particularly with unsupportive senior management, may leave him open to feminisation.

That wardens and tutors are expected to respond parentally to un-ruly students is supported in the *Times Higher Education Supple-ment's* coverage of the suggestion that universities deploy antisocial behaviour orders (ASBOs) against disruptive students in halls (North, 2005:19). At present, ASBOs are only available to police, local councils and housing associations. A warden at a pre-1992 univer-sity comments in this report: 'we try to use a tough-minded but tender-hearted approach'. The author sums up such concerns as indicating the intention of many universities to be: 'sympathetic to students' need for space to develop into adults'. This takes us back to Race's (2001) contention (see Chapter Three) that students are rebels. Students are being viewed as teenagers who have just broken free from mummy's apron-strings and are indulging in fairly incon-sequential and short-lived bad behaviour such as drinking exces-sively. The deployment of ASBOs against hall residents has yet to be carefully considered but infantilising students and not making them responsible for their actions is inappropriate and unhelpful for everyone concerned. In contrast to the rather cosy university staff quoted in the piece, a lawyer remarks tellingly that: 'maybe univer-sities are in denial...' (North, 2005:19).

Discussion

Unacceptable student conduct and unhelpful managerial interven-tion are not, then, just problems for women academics – men can be victims too. They are not sex-specific but neither are they gender-neutral, as early workplace bullying researchers like Adams (1992) argued. Taking the 'everyone can be a victim' approach could under-mine the acknowledging of sexism's role in student misconduct and in managerial intervention. Sexism is clearly a major factor and gender-neutrality does not stand up to analysis. This chapter shows that even if men and women are encountering experiences of student misconduct and managerial intervention of a similar nature, gender dynamics are part of every experience.

Steve, for instance who failed to provide resources for the students was finally rejected by them after he was seen in a feminised state, prompted by his medical condition. Sam found that what would usually be permitted from an older male teacher, a display of strict fatherly authority, students did not accept from a newly-appointed older male academic. The male dean's emphasis upon what he perceived as Ben's intention to 'defraud the faculty' indicates discomfort with the idea of such a teacher being threatened by a younger male student. Brian's 'feminised' learning and teaching methods, juxtaposed with his more 'masculine' detachment from students, meant that he was not the 'nurturing father' the students engaged in student-centred learning may have expected, and senior managers at Edward's university seemed to want him to be the authoritarian father keeping the children under control in the hall.

The gender dynamics relating to older academic men's experiences of student conduct and managerial intervention are relevant to the rest of this book. In particular, the emphasis upon discourses of fathering demonstrates a similarity with the earlier analysis of academic women's experiences of 'compulsory motherwork' (Cummins, 2005). Thus, although 'feminist analysis is certainly broad enough to account for men who do not fit the traditional construction of man' (Samuels, 2003:479) and men who fit the traditional construction of man might not be accommodated, a place must be made for all mistreated academic men in feminist theory and practice. We have to acknowledge and respond to men's gendered oppression.

While recognising that academic men can be subjects of oppression, it is essential that: 'oppression of men, if we recognise it, in no way detracts from the serious and horrible nature of the oppression of women' (New, 2001:743). Indeed, a recognition of the oppression of academic men should never be taken to mean that the structural nature of academic women's oppression in higher education is the same as this. Acker and Armenti (2004:20) have observed that because women are outsiders in academia they are 'subject both to a felt need to prove themselves up to the task and to the contradictory and conflicted expectations of colleagues and administrators'. Most male academics are still highly privileged (Morley, 1999) compared with most female. Tellingly, a university lecturer since the 1970s relates his frustration when the police did not seem to take his experiences of being stalked by a woman student seriously, because 'I was used to my words being given some credibility...' (Fine, 1997: 52).

The nature of women's oppression in wider society has also to be taken into account when looking at experiences in the academy. Emily described how she felt after the male student physically attacked her in the seminar room: 'I had to walk home in the dark. ... I thought he's going to wait outside for me and have another go at me'. The fear of rape is always present for academic women who are mistreated by male students, and although men do encounter rape (Lees, 1997), this would not be the major fear of a man faced with a problematic student.

Oppression is not 'normal' for women and 'more shocking and horrifying' (Gillespie, 1996:161) for men. But we should note that academic men can feel in danger of feminisation when they encounter unacceptable student conduct and insensitive managerial intervention. Steve constantly attempted to reclaim a 'masculine' identity during our interview; Sam's characterisation of the incident with the student as 'quite trivial and really rather pointless' typifies how men see themselves as forbidden to feel harmed by events. Brian's likening of a student complaint to 'a physical assault' can be seen as an attempt to underpin a masculine identity which has been shaken, and Edward consistently presented himself in the interview as powerful in relation to the unruly students. When prompted though, he admitted that he did not discuss his experiences in the hall with fellow academics through: '... fear of, I suppose, giving an impression that I couldn't handle it'. Ben's Dean of Faculty, meanwhile, exemplified another man's discomfort with the danger of feminisation.

Yet while these men can be said to have recognised, in different ways and to different degrees, that encountering bad behaviour from students might position them as not 'real men' (Lee, 2000b), the 'not a real man' discourse is a red herring, however potent it remains for many men (Stanko and Hobdell, 1993). We should simply see these men as having encountered experiences of unacceptable student conduct: they are no more 'not real men' than academic women who encounter such conduct are 'just girls who can't manage students'.

No younger academic men are included in the research. So are younger male academics encountering similar conduct and management, or do they feel unable to reveal such experiences, particularly to a female interviewer, because the dominant social construction of academic masculinity requires them to be: 'competitive, aggressive and individualistic' (Morley, 1999:84)? These questions remain to be explored.

Naming the problem

How should the experiences men and women have reported be conceptualised? Naming is important – it 'involves making visible what was invisible, defining as unacceptable what was acceptable and insisting that what was naturalised is problematic' (Kelly, 1988:139).

In Chapter Two, I used the term 'unacceptable student conduct' whilst noting that the respondents whose accounts were explored drew upon discourses of bullying and sexual harassment. It is a term I use regularly, for instance to recruit research participants, as the word 'unacceptable' instantly questions the widely-held, unproblematised assumption that students can behave how they choose. But it does not indicate that personal identities are relevant to unacceptable student conduct, nor is it especially catchy.

In Chapter Three, I used the interpretation for misconduct that is premised upon identity – essentially, gender identity – sexual harassment, and specifically contrapower sexual harassment, a term originating in the US. I interviewed women and men who found this interpretation useful. Others found the word 'contrapower' problematic because they conceptualised power in a particular way: one person has it so another does not, and they felt students are very powerful. Equally, 'sexual harassment' can be problematic terrain in which to locate a newly-identified social problem: despite its success (Brant and Too, 1994b), it is still not always recognised.

Chapter Four drew together the previous empirical chapters focusing upon women's experiences to locate unacceptable student conduct towards academic women in the context of sexism in the academy and suggested that we do not always need to employ the term 'sexual harassment' if we validate terms such as 'sexism' (Lee, 2001). This validation has, however, yet to be fully achieved.

The concept of 'workplace bullying' requires evaluation with reference to HE. Many of the academics interviewed for this research used this term, particularly where their experiences were not conventionally 'sexual'. The analysis developed in Chapters Two through Five has demonstrated how gender dynamics are implicated in such experiences; and while recognition of gender dynamics would, as Chapter One showed, have been highly contentious to the mainstream workplace bullying debate in the 1990s, today even though critical mass in this area has not yet been achieved, space is being opened up for a recognition of the salience of personal identities to workplace bullying. Workplace bullying is becoming a discourse in which feminist social scientists can and should engage, in order to provide academic analyses and practical interventions.

Bullying has been revealed to be a significant problem in universities – a context where many feminist social scientists work. A survey commissioned by the *Times Higher Education Supplement* (*THES*) 'elicited an unprecedented response from the academic community' (Lipsett, 2005:1): over 700 self-selecting academics identified themselves as encountering workplace bullying. Their experiences ranged from 'being shouted and sworn at in front of others, to having promotion blocked to being isolated from colleagues' (Lipsett, 2005:1). Feminist analyses of workplace bullying could contribute to the disruption of the victim-blaming approach in much workplace bullying research. This is needed in the contemporary academy. The researcher commissioned by the *THES* to conduct the survey reported that, 'usually with a survey, people question your methods or findings. They don't criticise your participants', yet in this study people wrote to say that academic workplace bullying victims were 'whiny, oversensitive people who can't hack it ... they claim they're bullied when they've done a crap job' (Boynton, 2005: 16).

Conventional wisdom in academia tends to insist that problems with students are the fault of the academic concerned whereas the evidence presented here is that academics who encounter unacceptable student conduct are unexceptional. This chapter has given instances of what conventional wisdom would read as academic responsibility: Steve said his performance was affected by overwork and Sam noted that he should not have been teaching a particular aspect of Economics. This enables important points to be made: even if problems have occurred, staff should not be treated badly by students or managers, for problems are frequently the responsibility of institutions and managers rather than the fault of individual academics.

The unsympathetic characterisations of bullied academics Boynton received, however, imply that while many university staff may wish to adopt the workplace bullying discourse to describe their experiences, 'workplace bullying' may be a difficult concept to deploy successfully in HE today, where 'the myth of meritocracy' (Morley, 1999:166) retains a disappointing currency. A concept with connotations of children in playgrounds may be insufficiently powerful to disrupt this entrenched and unhelpful way of thinking.

The concept of 'violence at work' may offer a more suitable interpretation of unacceptable student conduct. Hearn and Parkin (2001: 65) make the point that the discourse of workplace (physical) violence 'is, like bullying, usually not specifically gendered...'. Victims of violence, just like victims of any oppression, can encounter victim-blaming. My intention, as discussed in Chapter Six, is to propose a campaign against unacceptable student conduct and insensitive managerial intervention, and I agree with Kitzinger (1994: 130) that 'definitions are socially constructed to serve specific political ends'. For a campaign, a catchy label is required to raise awareness of problems generally swept under the carpet. The NHS zero tolerance zone campaign has certainly raised awareness of mistreatment of NHS staff by non-staff with its focus upon 'violence', and there is already one precedent for referring to the problems academics can encounter from students as 'occupational violence'. In their analysis of student aggression in tertiary education in Australia, Mayhew *et al* (2003) use the term 'occupational violence'.

The suggestion is not that terms such as contrapower sexual harassment, sexism, bullying, homophobia, anti-lesbianism, disablism, racism and ageism should be placed under an umbrella term of 'violence in higher education'. That would be to deny the specificities of particular discourses, such as that 'sexual harassment' clearly highlights the unwanted male sexual conduct women routinely encounter; and that 'workplace bullying' raises awareness of abuse of organisational power. Such an umbrella term would also take away the right of academics to develop their own interpretations of what has happened to them. In earlier work in the field of sexual harassment (Lee, 2001), I argued that a range of different interpretations rather than just the one – 'sexual harassment' – need to be available so that more women can firmly conceptualise unwanted male conduct as unacceptable.

The term 'violence in higher education' should be the leading campaigning tool against unacceptable student conduct and subsequent managerial intervention. But the discourses of unacceptable student conduct, contrapower sexual harassment, sexism, bullying, racism, homophobia, anti-lesbianism, disablism and ageism should remain equally valid. Academics should not feel that they have to choose a single discourse when confronted with students and managers behaving badly. For as Kitzinger (1994:133) notes: 'oppressions are not additive, but interactive' and that the discourse a victim highlights 'may depend on her audience'. Right now the audience of UK universities needs to be required to recognise the sorts of experiences described in this book, and 'violence in higher education' is the powerful interpretation this audience should hear. But as Kitzinger (p131) argues: 'we should not allow ourselves to be forced into the position of trying to construct and defend watertight, once-and-for-all, 'accurate' definitions'. The character of UK universities may change sufficiently for alternative ways of conceptualising students and managers behaving badly to be developed. Terms such as 'conflicts' or 'disputes' might be preferred to 'violence'. The discourse can only develop once a campaign against the problems identified in this book is underway. The next chapter proposes the nature of this campaign.

6
Taking action

Seldom are social problems easily resolved. But steps can be taken to deal with violence in HE and this chapter suggests some approaches and strategies. The *THES* has made a valuable contribution to raising awareness of this newly-identified social problem in HE and this should now be translated into action. A campaign would involve promoting self-help activities, commissioning institutional audits, conducting risk assessments, implementing personal safety measures, revising policies and procedures and providing networking and development opportunities for staff and students.

The practical section of the chapter draws on two models: the zero tolerance zone campaign against violence to staff working in the National Health Service, praised by healthcare professionals beyond the UK such as Jackson *et al* (2002), and the Union of Shop, Distributive and Allied Workers (USDAW) freedom from fear campaign, which promotes respect for UK retail employees. The publicity materials for the NHS campaign declare that: 'staff working in the NHS should not have to experience violence and abuse at work – it does not go with the job...' (Department of Health, 1999:9). The USDAW (2002:1) press release states that 'the customer is not always right'. Neither should it be part of the job of university employees to have to experience violence, even when students are interpreted as consumers.

If it is to succeed, however, any campaign must be underpinned by effective university management. The importance of managers is stressed in the NHS zero tolerance zone campaign: managers are told that they 'have a key role to play'. We have seen that in HE managers do not always play a key role, and often undermine staff. There is a need for management to have training about violence. Given the current character of UK higher education, however, significant cultural change is required before the problems revealed in this book can be addressed.

Practical responses to violence in higher education

We have seen that the workers defined as most at risk from violence are: 'those who are engaged in giving a service, caring, education, cash transactions, delivery/collection, controlling and representing authority' (Health and Safety Executive, 2004:1). The British Crime Survey (BCS) for 2002-2003 (Upson, 2004) shows that people in protective service occupations such as police officers, fire-fighters and prison officers are most at risk of assaults and threats at work, followed by health and welfare associate professionals. Obviously, academics do not fit these categories but what they do is consistent with the HSE definition of a risky occupation. Academics are working in education, seeking to care for students, and are often seen by students as representing authority. And we know that they encounter violence at work.

At present most university staff are insufficiently aware that students can behave violently. This means that when they or their colleagues experience abuse it is generally conceptualised as an individual problem rather than a collective one. Similarly people who encountered workplace bullying often initially conceptualised that problem in self-destructive ways, blaming themselves for the bad behaviour of others (Liefooghe and Olafsson, 1999). There are lessons from the theory and practice of feminism:

> The process of getting together with other women to talk openly and validate each other's experiences frees us from the notion that the 'truth' about our reality can be given only from above, by those with power over us, the experts. By telling our own stories of our reality, in our own words, we achieve a sense of autonomy... (Körner, 2002:129)

I mentioned that the academics who were interviewed were delighted that students' bad behaviour was the subject of a research project. They were pleased to discover that they were not alone in encountering such behaviour. When I presented my first conference paper on 'interpersonal abuse in higher education' (Lee, 2002b), the academics present expressed surprise at the idea that they could conceptualise behaviour problems as 'unacceptable'. They hadn't realised they could object to being treated badly: it had seemed to be part of the job. This response is common among workers. The academics at my presentation were prompted to review previously under-problematised interactions with students: what had been for them an individual problem became a collective, social problem.

All academics need to have the opportunity to review how they are treated by students and to decide if they wish to conceptualise particular interactions as unacceptable and not as part of the job. This is not a straightforward matter. The shame felt by workplace bullying victims in further and higher education is typified by one woman who had been bullied by a superior in higher education, demanding of a researcher: 'How can I go to personnel and say that I am being bullied? This is a university. We are supposed to be able to cope with this sort of thing' (Lewis, 2004:292). The feeling that professional people should be able to cope with misconduct is often heightened when those behaving unacceptably are below the victim in the organisational hierarchy. In such circumstances, professional identity can be seriously compromised. This point was underlined by Brian (Chapter Five): 'it didn't feel particularly that this was something we could talk about and get assistance with ... it just spreads the version around that you are not as good as you think you are'. Brian is correct: this is what currently happens. Until a campaign against violence in HE, is underway academics should proceed very carefully when raising concerns about student conduct – unless they have exceptionally enlightened managers and colleagues.

The largely hidden nature of problems with students, the prevalence of the view that staff who encounter them are inadequate or inexperienced, and the need to challenge these views made me place my research in the public domain as soon as I could. I wanted to contribute to the recognition of a social problem and challenge the idea that 'whatever happens in your classroom is your own fault' – how Josephine's line manager responded when she encountered problems with students. I submitted an article to the *THES*.

Wise and Stanley (1987:24) state that: "recognition' of something as a 'social problem' can be by a collectivity ... or by individuals who in some way have 'clout" and clearly the *THES* has 'clout'. They put this clout to getting student violence towards academics recognised as a social problem. Not only did they welcome my feature article but the topic made the front page. This feature and news story and a second front page news story in 2004 in which I was quoted, raised awareness of ways in which students behave inappropriately towards academics. My conference presentations (2002b, 2004, 2005a), a journal article (2005b) and this book contribute to this awareness-raising exercise. As a result, many academics have now been alerted to the fact that women and men in universities can experience stalking, physical and verbal attacks, sexual remarks made in person, by telephone/email, disrespect in the classroom, and accusations of inadequate teaching or supervision delivered in student evaluation questionnaires or directly to managers. They have seen that managers are not always supportive, and most importantly, they have been encouraged not to accept management interventions which are premised upon blaming them – the victims.

But this is not to say that recognition of violence in HE is now achieved, or that progress thus far has been unproblematic. A doctoral candidate wrote an unsympathetic response in the Letters pages of the *THES* to my article of 2003. Dempsey (2003) contended that my research was a 'fantasy' and said that: 'if students fail to respect lecturers, it might be because they think academic staff such as the ones in this article are too unthinking, immature or prejudiced towards them to merit much respect'. Sexual harassment was treated in this way in the UK in the 1980s. After initially sympathetic coverage, the press started presenting the sexual harasser as 'a man engaging in normal male responses to a sexual situation' (Wise and Stanley, 1987:32). Dempsey's letter presents unacceptable student conduct as just part of the job. Raising the problem is seen as showing contempt for students, just as highlighting sexual harassment was viewed in the 1980s as showing a disregard for 'normal' workplace interaction. Happily, unsympathetic responses to the problem of violence in HE have not yet been widespread, although they may well increase as the profile of this issue rises.

The profile of violence in higher education needs to be raised via a campaign along the lines of the NHS zero tolerance zone campaign and the freedom from fear campaign. The NHS campaign was prompted by research conducted by the NHS Executive revealing that: 'seven violent incidents were recorded each month per 1,000 staff. This is equivalent to approximately 65,000 violent incidents against NHS Trust staff each year' (Department of Health, 1999:4). Similarly, statistics revealing significant violence against shop workers informed the freedom from fear campaign. As this book focuses upon the experiences of twenty academics, it may be perceived as too small in scale to initiate a national campaign.

However, my research has prompted the *THES* to use the Freedom of Information Act to request data from universities about student violence against staff. The results (Baty, 2005:1) show that 'over the past five years, universities and colleges have recorded more than 1,000 incidents of student aggression towards staff'. This confirmed my suspicions: my twenty informants are the tip of an iceberg. Clearly, more quantitative and qualitative surveys and studies are required to extend the analysis but Baty's statistics, along with my qualitative data which makes clear the destructiveness of student violence on staff morale, means that there is now sufficient information available to try to set up a campaign against violence in UK higher education.

The campaign should involve not just the higher education press but trade unions and universities. The Association of University Teachers (AUT) and the National Association of Teachers in Further and Higher Education (NATFHE) have already shown interest in my research. Partnership working is vital for successful campaigning (USDAW, 2002).

The NHS and USDAW campaigns provide models of strategy. The HE campaign should also use posters, resource packs, a practical focus upon violence reduction and prevention strategies, and support for staff who have been mistreated. Some of the literature need only be adapted: for example, the NHS resource pack declares:

> Staff working in the NHS should not have to experience violence and abuse at work – it does not go with the job and is destructive on many levels. It diverts attention away from patients. It dampens morale, wastes resources and causes inefficiencies. As well as putting off potential new recruits, existing staff are more likely to throw in the towel. Health care professionals do not come to work to be victims. The NHS zero tolerance campaign is aimed at ridding the NHS of intimidation and violence. (Department of Health, 1999: 9)

The universities campaign, too, would stress that 'we don't have to take this'. This would reassure staff already affected and introduce the unacceptability of student violence to all members of staff. They should understand why the interpretation 'violence' has been chosen. It is a powerful campaigning term which, as in the NHS campaign, should not be taken to refer only to physical attack. Violence can encompass what staff may prefer to call unacceptable student conduct, contrapower sexual harassment, sexism, racism, anti-lesbianism, homophobia, ageism, disablism and bullying.

Information is only the start. The campaign should follow the NHS model, adapting its aim: 'to get over to the public that violence against staff working in the NHS is unacceptable and the Government and the NHS is determined to stamp it out' (Department of Health, 1999:4). The freedom from fear campaign is equally emphatic (USDAW, 2002). Students, their families and wider society need to be made aware that a problem has been recognised and that action is being taken to deal with it. Current and prospective students must be given this message, just as patients in the NHS are told that 'aggression, violence and threatening behaviour will not be tolerated any longer' and customers in shops informed that '[violence and abuse] cannot be tolerated. Shop workers must be allowed to go to work with freedom from fear'.

Everyone in or entering university must be made aware that there is a change in what is considered acceptable conduct towards university staff. It should be underlined that students are not customers who are always right. Instead, they are involved in a 'partnership approach [with obligations on both sides] ... rather than a commercial consumer approach' (Palfreyman and Warner, 1998). Academics should no longer feel that: '... [students] think you're at their beck and call. ... we've got to be very careful, because we have a student charter and they can say 'you weren't there when I came to see you' and we can be in all sorts of disciplinary problems' (Baron, 2000:157). This is no longer acceptable.

The process of awareness-raising in external constituencies must be done in a 'tactful and user-friendly manner which does not antagonise' (Fleming and Harvey, 2002:231). Current students should be involved in developing strategies for raising awareness among their peers. They should stress that the campaign is not to undermine student rights, neither is it making professionals unaccountable, but that it seeks to promote an atmosphere of mutual respect in the academic community by raising the profile of staff rights which, unlike student rights, have still to be properly recognised. Students can certainly be reminded of their own rights, and can be advised that they have recourse to the Office of the Independent Adjudicator (www.oia.ac.uk) if they have a complaint which they feel has not been effectively resolved internally.

In a climate of greater awareness, staff who have been harmed by violence might wish to establish self-help groups, in and even beyond their universities. When 'workplace bullying' was first named in the UK in the early 1990s victims of workplace bullying sought support, and self-help groups proved useful. Troman describes a teacher self-help group he attended while researching teacher stress. The group was established to support teachers who had encountered bullying from headteachers and drew members from the area, not just the school. Members related how they were bullied, and 'some talked at length of the trauma of the experience and its aftermath' (Troman, 2003:151). Fellow members would share their own experiences and offer advice. The group provided social events and considered which therapies might be useful.

Self-help groups offer a community of people with similar experiences and a relatively safe setting in which to embark upon the journey from victim to survivor. But the groups must take care not to leave problems individualised and thus perpetuate people's vulnerability: individual experiences need to be interpreted as collective, social problems. Given that violence in higher education is a newly-identified problem, self-help may best be targeted specifically for academics who have been mistreated by students and the groups established may meet or be conducted through the internet. And there are existing help mechanisms for educators, such as the Teacher Support Network, which academics might draw on. This provides a telephone counselling service, Teacher Support Line, and a confidential interactive service, Teacher Support Online. Information is available from www.teachersupport.info.

The next step must be to ensure that all higher education institutions start taking proper responsibility for the welfare of their staff, in respect of violence from students. The law is in place: 'employers have a legal duty [under the Health and Safety at Work Act 1974] to ensure, so far as is reasonably practicable, the health, safety and welfare at work of their employees' (HSE, 2004). Universities must also apply their understanding of legislation relating to equality, such as the Sex Discrimination Act, to violence from students. Thirty-seven respondents to Baty's (2005) Freedom of Information Act request had no record of violence towards staff, whereas others had details of up to two hundred incidents in the five year reporting period. Baty's findings imply that either many universities are entirely free from staff-student problems, which is doubtful, or that not all higher education institutions are taking the health, safety and welfare of their employees with regard to student violence seriously. Universities which have no idea of how many staff are being mistreated by students, in which ways, and with what consequences, must be urged to conduct audits. Even universities which do have more realistic statistics would benefit from audits. They may find that there is more going on than reporting procedures have so far revealed. Audits should be conducted by external consultants so that the process remains fair and impartial. But Ishmael (1999:151-2) warns that surveys: 'can either encourage [staff] to be open and honest about their experiences, or make them wary or cautious about their responses'.

Before they conduct audits, institutions must make their staff aware of the problems of student-perpetrated violence, unacceptable conduct, contrapower sexual harassment, sexism, racism, anti-lesbianism, homophobia, ageism, disablism and bullying. If awareness has not been raised, staff may persist in believing that anything short of a physical attack is just part of the job and that it is an admission of inadequacy to report student abuse, even in a confidential survey. Once awareness is raised, however, audits may reveal a wide range of problematic experiences encountered by academics.

When higher education institutions are more aware of the problems their staff encounter from students, risk assessments should be revisited or initiated if they are not already in place. Risk assessment is a significant aspect of the NHS zero tolerance zone campaign, consistent with the Management of Health and Safety at Work Regulations (1999), which say that 'employers must assess the risks to employees and make arrangements for their health and safety by effective planning, organisation, control, monitoring and review' (HSE, 2004:2). Higher education institutions should review whether their environments may 'trigger or exacerbate a stressful situation' as the DOH (1999:6) warns.

Many HE staff and students currently operate in conditions which are not ideal. For instance, we saw Sally threatening that if action was taken regarding a claim of plagiarism: 'she knew that Megan parked her car in the badly-lit car park behind the business studies building and often worked late at night. She would be waiting for her in that car park', and Helen felt threatened when she had to teach an evening class in an isolated temporary classroom, knowing that Sally would wait for her. Should academics be required to use badly-lit car parks or teach evening classes in isolated classrooms? Helen's and Megan's physical environment exacerbated their feelings of insecurity when they encountered a problematic student. Had they been NHS employees, these issues would probably have been recognised and resolved.

Risk assessments can also be deployed to develop safety strategies for communications between staff, as advised in the NHS. One strategy they and USDAW suggest is provision of panic buttons. USDAW advocates that: 'it should be possible to operate the button unobtrusively when staff feel under threat. The button should trigger a remote alarm and not an alarm on the spot. There must be reliable procedures for prompt assistance to be provided when the alarm is triggered' (2002:2). If panic buttons and other communications strategies, such as mobile phones, are being provided elsewhere, why not in universities? In the NHS, funding has been made available for safety measures and this should be considered in the HE sector. If there had been panic buttons in the accommodation where Emily, Helen and Stella were physically attacked by students, every one of them could have called for assistance. Furthermore, the very existence of panic buttons would have heightened their awareness of the possibility of student violence. Until panic buttons are installed, staff should memorise the number for security at their institutions and keep their mobile phones to hand.

Policies also raise awareness. In early 2002, I analysed university websites to determine whether recognition of unacceptable student conduct towards academics was featured in university personnel policies and I discovered that awareness of the problem was scant. Further analysis via a short email questionnaire sent to personnel professionals at 95 UK universities drew a disappointing response, even after an email reminder accompanied by a second copy of the questionnaire. Sixty-four universities did not respond. Eleven declined to participate. Twenty questionnaires were received, twelve from pre-1992 universities and eight from post-1992 universities. The completed questionnaires revealed that ten of the pre-1992 universities and five of the post-1992 universities did not explicitly mention student harassment of staff in their personnel policies: in the remaining five it was mentioned, but not in a separate policy.

However, five of the pre-1992 universities and three of the post-1992 universities (40%) said they would consider a separate policy to highlight unacceptable student conduct towards staff. There should now be clear 'unacceptable student conduct' policies in all universities and these should be made accessible via personnel websites, where they should be positioned along with harassment, bullying and grievance policies which focus upon problems between co-workers and managers.

Personnel professionals, trade union representatives, health and safety advisors, academics, managers and students should all be asked for input in developing 'unacceptable student conduct' policies. The importance of including a wide range of people is stressed in the NHS campaign: 'involving staff in drawing up local policies is essential, not only do they have a vested interest but their direct involvement will help ensure their support'. Thomas's (2004) survey of sexual harassment policies in the UK confirms the value of working groups in the development of policies:

> 'Top-down' policies tend to convey the message that harassment is essentially an individual problem involving interpersonal conflict which, if sufficiently troublesome, can be arbitrated by one's employer ... By contrast, the message 'consultative' policies generally convey is that a climate in which harassment exists is detrimental to the university community at large, thereby constructing harassment as more than just an individual problem. (Thomas, 2004:153)

A 'consultative' approach is highly appropriate for policy development in the area of student violence because problems with students are so often interpreted as individual failings.

Working groups must start by considering what sorts of experiences might be reported under the policy. The definition of violence adopted by the NHS encompasses verbal abuse as well as physical violence. NHS staff still might only report verbal abuse they feel is 'serious' – what Wise and Stanley (1987) call 'sledgehammer' experiences. As we try to increase understanding of occupational violence, staff in all occupations should raise concerns about a wide range of incidents: violence research demonstrates that a hierarchy of seriousness cannot be meaningfully constructed because people are differently affected by incidents. Less 'serious' incidents that Wise and Stanley (1987) call 'dripping tap' experiences should also be reported because as, Ishmael (1999:52) observes:

> In many instances there will be an escalating pattern of violence, which may start with verbal abuse and proceed to physical attack. Unless the initial verbal abuse is recorded, an organisation could miss the opportunity to prevent any escalation.

A broad definition of violence in higher education would provide a picture of what it is like to operate in this sector. The wide-ranging data produced could be used to keep risk assessments and safety measures under review. Record-keeping is certainly important to provide statistics but there is a need to have: 'effective incident report processes and analysis of these reports [which] can increase awareness of how to avoid potentially violent situations and deal effectively with aggressive patients [or students]' (McKenna *et al*, 2003:62).

To construct effective policy the procedures that are adopted are crucial. A network of trained harassment advisors is needed, who can give advice informally. In the mid-1990s, when Thomas (2004) conducted her survey of sexual harassment policies in the UK, she found that 67 per cent of the universities responding had a network of harassment advisors and that those who did so and who had developed their policy via consultation had higher reporting rates of sexual harassment. This illustrates the value of informal contacts, and collaborative not top-down policy. Where there are no harassment advisors, the first point of contact for staff who have been mistreated would be their line manager, personnel department or trade union representative but, as Thomas (2004:153) says, this is liable to be 'more off-putting to potential users'.

The Department of Health advocates 'robust, uncomplicated reporting systems' for making formal reports of violence. Staff are encouraged to record the details of the individuals involved, when/where the incident happened, triggers for the incident, any injuries sustained and any absence as a result, and, importantly, 'the action taken by managers to prevent the incident occurring again' (1999:7). The reporting forms should be easily available in paper copies and to download from university websites. They need to be clear about how to complete them and where to send them next.

The policy must make clear what will happen once a concern has been raised. People who are violent to NHS staff are given verbal and then written warnings. If verbal or written warnings are given to HE students, staff who remain intimidated by a particular student or students should not be expected to continue to teach them. Teaching is stressful enough, and standing alone in front of a class containing an intimidating student who has been reprimanded may be a threatening prospect. Academics should not be victimised if they make a complaint, nor be expected to be grateful for being 'permitted' to do so. In circumstances where written and verbal warnings are inadequate, such as when a physical attack has taken place, universities, like hospitals, need to have effective contacts with the police and prosecution services.

As in the NHS, so in HE it must be understood that students may behave inappropriately as a consequence of mental health conditions. Higher education is changing: Helen's and Megan's problems with Sally cannot be written off as isolated incidents. The Association for University and College Counselling (1999:1) reports that 'there is broad agreement from counselling services that the severity of emotional and behavioural disturbance among university students is increasing' and they observe that support services have not been adequately expanded to take account of widening participation initiatives and 'this has resulted in greater pressure being placed upon existing services and academic and administrative staff'.

Universities UK offer mental health guidelines to vice-chancellors, principals and senior managers responsible for strategic planning and resource allocation. It is advised that when students are threatening fellow students and staff, there should be procedures whereby they can suspend their studies.

Once a policy has been drawn up it must be thoroughly disseminated. Rayner *et al* (2002:167) note that although an [anti-bullying] policy can simply be circulated on paper, 'it is much safer to allow for interpersonal contact through launch events'. Attending such events should not be voluntary because everyone needs to be aware of the policy and to know that a senior person in the university is accountable for it and will be reporting back upon progress. USDAW recommend that 'a named senior manager (e.g. HR director) should have operational responsibility for putting the policy into practice'.

The launch of the policy should be followed by continuing professional development (CPD). Many of the academics whose experiences have been explored in this book did not know what to do when students abused them. This is consistent with the experiences of many workers.

However, a call for CPD with regard to violence has to be made carefully. Unhelpfully, self-help manuals about personal safety often require workers to look after themselves:

> The focus is not on the violator, the propensity of certain people to be violent, on the workers themselves as violent, on social divisions, such as gender, not on the greater risk elsewhere, such as at home – but on the potentially violated person who is given the responsibility to keep themselves safe. (Hearn and Parkin, 2001:70)

The staff development proposals made here are not simplistically about making university staff responsible for their own safety. As we can learn from the NHS campaign: 'training is *only one element* of a prevention strategy. Effective training should support other systems and should not be relied upon as the only means of dealing with violence at work'.

There should be opportunities for early career academics and post-graduates who teach to discuss the problems they are encountering in academic life, with particular reference to interactions with students. This need is indicated in the interviews in Chapter Two: Eve, for instance, said that she would be reluctant to talk about unacceptable student conduct in case she was seen to be incompetent. So, clearly, safe spaces need to be created for discussion of problems with students.

Peer networking for graduate students has been found helpful. A feminist research group for women Psychology graduate students, for example, decided to conduct a group research project on feminist women's experiences in graduate school. In their meetings: 'sexism was discussed at great length. We talked about sexist encounters with students in our roles as graduate assistants, with teaching assistants that were assigned to us, and with professors and peers' (Barata *et al*, 2005:240).

Peer mentoring for early career academics is examined via a scheme established at Purdue University Calumet. It was found that traditional mentoring is not always helpful to new faculty, because they 'can feel like graduate students with an advisor [supervisor]' (Osgood Smith *et al*, 2001:198). So peer mentoring can be more helpful. The head of school set up 'a collegial support group for new faculty – a networking group of individuals who share experiences and, by so doing, act as mentors for each other' (p200). The intention was that the participants prepare for promotion and tenure. Participants noted that they felt supported. Such peer networking and mentoring, with a focus on violence, may be useful to post-graduates who teach and to early career academics. This is not to say that such experiences cannot be helpfully explored via networking with and mentoring by more experienced faculty but so far many have a record of viewing staff problems with student abuse as due to inexperience or, as time passes, incompetence.

The problem of violence in HE needs to be introduced into teacher training courses and postgraduate certificate in learning and teaching programmes. As in the NHS, staff should have opportunities not just to learn how to defuse tension and to avoid physical attacks but also to explore reasons why violence may occur. They can learn from Dooris's qualitative study of students at a UK university, for instance, which reveals that students experience:

> Lack of money, time, information and advice, [and that they are] eating poorly and living generally unhealthy lifestyles, and experienc-

ing a wide range of symptoms such as headaches, irregular sleeping patterns, allergies and relationship problems. (Dooris, 1999:37)

Kuhlenschmidt and Layne (1999) highlight how difficulties of this nature can affect students' civility towards academic staff (see Mayhew *et al*, 2003 for a similar analysis). They also draw attention to environmental factors which affect student behaviour – for instance: 'large classes may encourage students to act as if they were in a movie theatre or watching television' (p53). None of this excuses bad behaviour – although students' problems should be addressed – but it helps academics realise they are not always to blame for difficulties with students. This is the most vital aspect of the staff development required.

While there is no: 'recipe for successful interpersonal relationships' because: 'there are too many variables in any circumstance to achieve perfection' (Kuhlenschmidt and Layne, 1999:55), a checklist approach to dealing with difficult students is not recommended. These authors seem to collude with the conventional wisdom in academia on problematic staff-student interaction. They ask academics to reflect upon their own behaviour when problems with students have arisen, because: 'you will be a better mediator if you examine your behaviour from the perspective of the student' (p48). Although it is always useful for professionals to reflect upon their own conduct and the power dynamics which operate in their field, this should be private and not lay them open to victim-blaming by managers.

I want academics to be enabled to keep their confidence and self-esteem when students and managers behave badly to them. This book will be useful for staff development because of its analysis of the structural nature of violence in higher education and the challenge to it being individualised. The book will enable newer academics to understand the relevance of their personal identities, academic status and disciplines in the students' responses. I hope they will be encouraged early in their careers not to blame themselves or accept blame from students or managers when problems arise. The current practice of blaming staff for problems with students means that academics need to consider how to protect themselves from inappropriate managerial intervention. For example, keeping evidence of positive feedback from students can be useful for an academic to quote in the event of a badly-managed complaint.

Staff development on the subject of violence in HE should not be restricted only to new faculty because more experienced staff experience abuse too. Academics often think that violence 'won't happen to me', but need to think instead it has not happened *yet*.

Everyone who encounters students must be urged or even required to participate in staff development on dealing with violence. The topics introduced to new faculty are just as relevant here. Kuhlenschmidt and Layne (1999:56) suggest that: 'personal characteristics, such as being female, being small, having a soft voice, or being shy, may increase your challenges when dealing with disruptive behaviour'. They propose that such staff find a similarly-placed colleague with whom to discuss coping strategies – thus further pathologising the individuals.

Everyone needs to be made aware of the dynamics of violence from students: feminists may encounter anti-feminism, women may experience sexism, Black men and women may encounter racism, men and women with disabilities may experience disablism, lesbian and gay staff may encounter anti-lesbianism and homophobia and that men who are white, heterosexual, middle-class and non-disabled may experience problems to do with their personal identities. Staff need to be given the conceptual tools to understand their own experiences: analysis of identities is crucial.

If all staff are involved they can not only explore theoretical understandings of violence but also develop practical, everyday measures such as mechanisms for sharing information. If students have been difficult in one module, other staff who will teach them need to be prepared. The sharing of information would help underdmine the individualisation of problems with student behaviour. Experiences of teaching also need to be shared. The individualisation of problems with students feeds on a situation about which Eve remarked perceptively: 'a great deal of what happens in university teaching is unspoken between colleagues'.

Staff CPD could also explore ways of supporting colleagues who encounter violence. 'Employees may need guidance and/or training to help them to react appropriately [to victims of work-related violence]' (HSE, 2004:10). Emily's colleagues laughed when she had been physically attacked by a student – staff generally remain longer than students so tensions generated by unhelpful responses must be avoided. Training is also important for trade union representatives and personnel officers who may receive complaints of student violence.

Support must be available for staff who have been subjected to violence. 'Rapid responses that aim to reduce possible adverse psychological consequences and the associated impacts on clinical practice' (McKenna *et al*, 2003:62) advocated for healthcare are equally appropriate for universities. Academics often feel undermined by the experience and this can affect future interactions with students in classrooms and beyond (McKinney and Crittenden, 1992). Formal counselling is generally available to staff in HE, but debriefing is less common and may often be all that is required. Secker *et al* (2004:177) advise that: 'to take account of individual coping styles psychological debriefing needs to be available, but not mandatory, for as long as required'. Eve's unease in class might have been resolved if she had been debriefed after she was shouted at: she wanted to discuss what had happened and needed to be reassured that it was the student who had behaved badly, not she who had responded incorrectly: she did what she could in the circumstances.

Students, in turn, need opportunities to think about their conduct towards university staff and this is for the universities to provide, as they are 'after all, educational institutions, with, one assumes, a belief in the value of education as a way of achieving beneficial change' (Carter and Jeffs, 1995:62). It cannot be assumed that all prospective and current students know how they should behave – as Tutors A and B (1996:1) explain, many believe that 'they are entering a bigger school to learn more difficult things. But higher education is not like school – it's very different'. It needs to be made clear to students what is expected of them as individuals, as well as what they should expect of staff as individuals. This book has shown students responding to academics in ways which draw inappropriately upon the actual or perceived personal identities of these staff. Walsh's (2005: 19) comment is relevant:

> Most young women and young men are denied an upbringing and education which provide them with an understanding of how they arrived at where they are now (individually and collectively as sexual and gendered beings), and the economic, social and cultural factors which continue to shape their lives and prospects as women and men (gay or straight). This results in ignorance and social vulnerability; and produces silence and conflict, where there should be discourse and dialogue.

These matters should be discussed prior to starting university, but current students too must be made aware of the dynamics of personal identities. They must be prepared to encounter a diverse range of teachers at university and must accept that a young female doctoral student facilitating a seminar is just as worthy of respect as an eminent male professor. Making equal opportunities awareness

more widespread in the academy may help to disrupt the vulnerability of feminist academics. Students must understand that
academics are not surrogate parents, but educators; and that whilst
they will usually be sympathetic to the students' stresses, the students must take responsibility for their own actions. If students fail
to honour the university's learning contracts or class ground rules
they should expect sanctions to be imposed.

Students should also be involved in discussing unacceptable conduct with their peers at induction and beyond: they are more likely
to listen to their peers than to a member of staff. There is a precedent
for this approach: students in the US are trained to offer induction
programmes which explore 'consensual' relationships between staff
and students on issues of discrimination, safety, health and well-
being (Carter and Jeffs, 1995). Students in the UK are rarely provided
with opportunities to consider 'consensual' relationships. So universities need to make students aware that just as it is unprofessional
for academics to initiate sexual relationships with them, it is inappropriate for students to sexualise academics, as we saw happened to Emily and Ben.

Once this process is underway, universities need to monitor the problem: Rayner *et al* (2002:167) say that monitoring should take place
every six months. Fleming and Harvey (2002:231) recommend a
bottom-up flow of information about violence at work. They say
that:

> The organisation needs to listen to all grades of staff on an ongoing
> basis, not only their perception and experience of violence, but also
> their perception of management responses, the adequacy of the
> organisation's efforts to address violence and the quality of educa-
> tion and training.

The importance of managers ... and the problem of new managerialism

Fleming and Harvey are right: management responses do need to be
monitored. The practical proposals made here have to be underpinned by appropriate university management. We have seen that
university managers can respond inappropriately to student abuse
of academics, and research tells us that managers frequently respond inappropriately to equal opportunities concerns. As Hearn
and Parkin (2001:54) report, victims of workplace sexual harassment, bullying and violence often 'find management actively com-
plicit or ignoring what happened'.

Equal opportunities concerns such as workplace sexual harassment, bullying and violence are usually understood to be about a superior attacking a subordinate. Possibilities for inappropriate managerial intervention in situations where the victim is a professional employee and the perpetrator a non-employee are greater still. This book has described many instances of university managers responding to student violence by blaming the academic subjected to it instead of disciplining the student.

Violence from students is unpleasant but I contend that the managerial intervention that follows is often more significant in disrupting academic careers. The response of managers to students behaving badly needs to change. The importance of managers was recognised in the NHS zero tolerance zone campaign. Its resources pack (1999) states that 'health service managers must do all they can to stop staff being assaulted and abused. *This issue must be at the top of the managerial agenda*' (p2 italics added). This must become a requirement in higher education also.

This book has recorded how the immediate line managers of Alison and Ben offered excellent support. But this is not the norm – continuing professional development is required for managers. While managers may believe that they do respond to issues of harassment, violence and inequality effectively, or would do if such problems arose, they do not always handle matters well. Case study research shows that even where managers viewed themselves in a positive light, staff raised concerns about 'aggressive management' (Deem, 2003:252). So all university managers may benefit from CPD to become more people-focused. And they need to be helped to realise that violence is not an individual problem but a collective, social problem. Seeing academics as wholly responsible for their own behaviour and the behaviour of others towards them is, an anti-feminist approach, so feminist consciousness-raising is important. As Johnson (2002:43) says: 'training needs to stimulate critical thought such that the old and new are both subject to interrogation, and to experimentation in relation to new contexts and circumstances'.

Not all training of managers takes such desirable approach: Deem and Johnson (2003) interviewed 137 university managers and discovered that few had experienced action learning. Many of the interviewees 'thought that managers were born, not made and saw management as common-sense'. The authors observe: 'the use of common-sense in relation to management can ... imply an over-simplified notion of management and an unreflective approach to tasks, processes and actions' (p8). Without proper training, blaming the person perceived as possessing power – the academic – will prevail.

Managers in the NHS are sent for the same training as their staff. This practice should be considered in HE, as managers could then explore issues with front-line academics, learn from their experiences and concerns and develop theoretical understandings of problems. Managers who are unaware of how to respond when an academic encounters violence and are open to reflecting upon these experiences and their own current practice would benefit from such CPD. Josephine's line manager blamed her initially but offered support after reading an article about unacceptable student conduct towards women. And male managers need to learn not to view women academics inappropriately as domestic figures such as mothers.

Managers need to learn how to treat academics fairly when students make allegations against them. The cases of Rachel, Josephine and Brian all showed that after a student has made a complaint, the academic wants to be kept informed. Complaints should certainly be investigated – professionals have to be accountable – but staff deserve to be treated with dignity and respect while this is taking place. Moreover, investigative procedures need to be and be seen to be fair. These points are taken up in the advice for NATFHE branches with regard to student complaints published in 2005 (available at: www. natfhe.org.uk). It contains a procedures checklist advising institutions 'to be alert to the personalisation of complaints that are in fact matters of corporate service provision rather than the responsibility of individual members of staff'. As the cases discussed in this book make clear, institutions should equally be alert to complaints prompted by the real or perceived personal identities of the staff concerned.

However, training for change will remain a difficult process in HE because not all university managers know how to respond appropriately when academics encounter violence from students. Those infected with new managerialism are likely to put financial considerations before the welfare of their staff. Deem (1998:48) explains that: 'the former polytechnics and colleges of higher education emerged from a rather more bureaucratically and hence more hierarchical and rule-bound local authority tradition than their more collegiate competitors' but notes that even in pre-1992 universities 'explicit management practices seem to be replacing rather more *laissez-faire* ways of organising...' (p48), often in response to external pressures. Such external pressures include 'the shift from elite to mass higher education [involving]... part-time students and the provision of 'access' for mature students' increased emphasis upon 'vocational training, work-related skills, and opportunities for life-long learning', 'the vexed issue of university funding', the 'shift away from allowing universities autonomy to regulate themselves and secure their own standards' and "marketisation' ... sweeping through universities as they struggle to enhance income to sustain their operations in the face of reductions in public funds' (Dearlove, 1997: 59). We saw evidence of some of these pressures in my case studies.

'Some manager-academics may be adept at using the current conditions to introduce cultural and other changes they would like to see, under the guise of having no choice' (Deem, 2003:255). And the new managerialism: 'offer[s] a new and unique opportunity [for managers] to engage in 'macho management' behaviour' (Kerfoot and Whitehead, 2000:198). People I interviewed for this book believed this to be true of higher education. 'Macho management' is not the preserve solely of male managers, although the bullying tactics deployed by men and women are generally of a gendered nature (Bray, 2001).

Managers in this era of managerialism may well claim to support a campaign against unacceptable student conduct. But Saunderson's analysis of women academics and new managerialism suggests otherwise. She notes the recent spate of equal opportunities initiatives, but argues that:

> Laudable as these initiatives are, unless they become an integral and intrinsic component, a part of the institutional culture of UK universities – then on the ground equal opportunities practice and experience will remain a nebulous and toothless concept ... A vigilant guard must be mounted against such initiatives being loudly applauded as excellent 'ideas' of good equal opportunities practice, and then framed and presented in Vice-Chancellors' offices around the country as self-certification and self-congratulatory portraits of 'sound EO policy' or, worse still, venerated and eulogized, then simply shelved and sidelined. (Saunderson, 2002:399-400)

Thomas (2004) indicates that this is already true of sexual harassment policies in universities. We might plead the business case for dealing appropriately with violence in higher education because 'new managerialism is supposed to be concerned with cost-effectiveness, yet occupational stress is not cost effective' (Morley, 2003:

79). But despite the business case for tackling sexual harassment, that problem still prevails in the academy.

If no other body takes an interest, the *THES* should ask for annual statistics on violence in higher education. If this is done while a campaign against this problem is running, many more incidents are sure to be reported, as happened in the NHS. Violent incidents in the NHS are being taken increasingly seriously: there were 759 prosecutions in 2004-5 compared with 51 in 2002-3 (BBC News Online, 2005). If more incidents in universities are reported and dealt with effectively and badly behaved students appropriately disciplined, we can be optimistic that the culture is beginning to change, not just because of the business case but because making staff welfare a low priority is becoming socially unacceptable. It is important to recognise that 'although universities are embracing a managerialism borrowed from business, the new academic managerialism is one that has been discredited in business' (Delanty, 2001:107). Dearlove (1997:69-70) identifies a positive model of management for the future:

> Blending collegiality and managerialism; striking balances between trust and control, between the need for teaching and research, and between the competing claims of different levels of organisation, ensuring that academic work is backed up by appropriate institutional incentives at the same time as academics are encouraged to look outside the university for funds and support, all call for difficult judgements and for complicated understandings of universities and academics. They call for a thinking organisational leadership that can map institutional complexity and put things together; that is as sensitive to the nature of academic work and academics as it is to the changing context within which universities are now having to organise; and that is prepared to work patiently with academics and others over time to steer major changes through a number of stages of decision and towards well-supported resolution and sustained implementation.

Summary

The *THES* has contributed to raising awareness of student violence towards academics as a newly-identified social problem in HE. This chapter proposes that awareness of the problem be developed by means of a campaign in HE. Appropriate measures would include promoting self-help activities, commissioning institutional audits, conducting risk assessments, implementing personal safety measures, revising policies and reporting procedures, and organising networking and development for staff and students. Previously-identified social problems such as sexual harassment and workplace bullying have been tackled in a similar way. As Wise and Stanley (1987:23) note, the final stage of the development of a social problem is often 'invisibility'. The practical measures explored here will be undermined if university managers are not made central to the campaign but this will not be easy in the prevailing university culture. We must hope that highlighting student violence and demanding that university staff be respected will challenge the *status quo*, but there are no quick fixes to the problems identified in this book.

End note

University Students Behaving Badly provides a feminist sociological analysis of student-perpetrated violence towards women and men academics in UK higher education. It analyses their experiences of physical attacks, stalking, verbal abuse, sexual remarks delivered in person, via email and anonymous telephone calls, complaints of poor teaching and supervision made in student feedback questionnaires or directly to university managers. And it explores the appalling ways in which some university managers have responded to incidents of this kind.

Rather than interpreting violence from university students as the responsibility of individual academics, researchers should realise that pathologising victims is unhelpful and also mistaken. Because *any* academic can be vulnerable to student-perpetrated violence and then face inappropriate managerial intervention.

Any academic, female or male, can be a victim but this does not mean that personal identities are irrelevant. Personal identities are never cast off when we enter the workplace: the dynamics of gender identity in academic women's and men's experiences of violence in higher education have been closely analysed.

This empirical analysis indicates the need for a campaign. The difficulties such a campaign is likely to encounter in an era of macho management have been exposed in this book and approaches suggested to overcome them.

Next, we require a quantitative survey exploring the prevalence of student-perpetrated violence in higher education to situate my qualitative claims in a wider picture. Tackling student violence merits more research projects and urgent action.

References

Abbas, A. and McLean, M. (2001) Becoming sociologists: professional identity for part-time teachers of university sociology. *British Journal of Sociology of Education*, 22 (3)

Acker, S. and Armenti, C. (2004) Sleepless in academia. *Gender and Education*, 16 (1)

Adams, A. (1992) *Bullying at work*, London: Virago

Adkins, L. (1995) *Gendered work*, Buckingham: Open University Press

Aitken, G. and Noble, K. (2001) Violence and violation: women and secure settings. *Feminist Review*, 68

Allen, L. (2005) Treat us fairly too. *The Lecturer*, October

Annandale, E. (1996) Working on the front line: risk culture and nursing in the new NHS. *Sociological Review*, 44 (3)

Association for University and College Counselling (1999) *Degrees of disturbance: the new agenda*, Rugby: British Association for Counselling

Atwood, J. (1994) Good intentions, dangerous territory: student resistance in feminist writing classes. *Journal of Teaching Writing*, 12

Barata, P., Hunjan, S. and Leggatt, J. (2005) Ivory tower? Feminist women's experiences of graduate school. *Women's Studies International Forum*, 28 (2)

Barnes-Powell, T. and Letherby, G. (1998) All in a day's work: gendered care work in higher education. In: Malina, D. and Maslin-Prothero, S. (eds) *Surviving the academy: feminist perspectives*, London: Falmer Press

Baron, H. (2000) Riding the crest of a trough: the commitment of academics in mass higher education. *Teacher Development*, 4 (1)

Baty, P. (2005) Violent students terrify staff. *Times Higher Education Supplement*, June 10th

BBC News Online (2005) Rise in charges over NHS assaults. August 29th. Available at http://news.bbc.co.uk. Accessed 29th August 2005

Becher, T. (1989) *Academic tribes and territories*, Buckingham: Open University Press

Benson, K.A. (1984) Comment on Crocker's 'An analysis of university definitions of sexual harassment'. *Signs*, 9

Bett Report (1999) *Independent review of higher education pay and conditions*, London: Stationery Office

Bhopal, K. (2002) Teaching women's studies: the effects of race and gender. *Journal of Further and Higher Education*, 26 (2)

Blaxter, L., Hughes, C. and Tight, M. (1998) *The academic career handbook*, Buckingham: Open University Press

Blaya, C. (2003) School violence and the professional socialisation of teachers. *Journal of Educational Administration*, 41 (6)

Boice, R. (1992) *The new faculty member*, Jossey Bass: Wiley

Boyd, C. (2002) Customer violence and employee health and safety. *Work, Employment and Society*, 16 (1)

Boynton, P. (2005) Time to tackle abuse head-on. *Times Higher Education Supplement*, September 16th

Brant, C. and Too, Y.L. (1994a) (eds) *Rethinking sexual harassment*, London: Pluto

Brant, C. and Too, Y.L. (1994b) Introduction. In Brant, C. and Too, Y.L. (eds) *Rethinking sexual harassment*, London: Pluto

Bray, C. (2001) Bullying nurses at work: theorising a gendered experience. *Contemporary Nurse*, 10

Brewis, J. and Linstead, S. (2000) *Sex, work and sex work*, London: Routledge

British Sociological Association (2002) Statement of ethical practice. www.brit-soc.co.uk. Accessed 21st December 2004

Brown, S. (2001) New at this. In: Edwards, H. Smith, B. and Webb, G. (eds) *Lecturing: case studies, experience and practice*, London: Kogan Page

Browne, J. and Russell, S. (2005) My home, your workplace: people with physical disability negotiate their sexual health without crossing professional boundaries. *Disability and Society*, 20 (4)

Carson, L. (2001) Gender relations in higher education: exploring lecturers' perceptions of student evaluations of teaching. *Research Papers in Education*, 16 (4)

Carter, P. and Jeffs, T. (1995) *A very private affair*, Derbyshire: Education Now

Chan, A. (2004) When women 'baby-sit' and men 'transmit knowledge and discipline': the construction of gender in Hong Kong's primary schools. *Equal Opportunities International*, 23 (3,4)

Cockburn, C. (1991) *In the way of women*, Basingstoke: Macmillan

Collins, S. and Parry-Jones, B. (2000) Stress: the perceptions of social work lecturers in Britain. *British Journal of Social Work*, 30 (6)

Committee of Vice-Chancellors and Principals (CVCP) [Now Universities UK] (1999) *Guidelines on student mental health policies and procedures for higher education*, London: CVCP

Cotterill, P. and Waterhouse, R. (1998) Women in higher education: the gap between corporate rhetoric and the reality of experience. In Danusia M. and Maslin-Prothero, S. (eds) *Surviving the academy: feminist perspectives*, London: Falmer Press

Coulter, R. (1995) Struggling with sexism: experiences of feminist first-year teachers. *Gender and Education*, 1

Coxon, K. (2002) Students get a lecture. *Education Guardian*, 16th July. Available at http://education.guardian.co.uk. Accessed 1st July 2005

Culley, M. (1985) Anger and authority in the introductory women's studies classroom. In Culley, M. and Portuges, C. (eds) *Gendered subjects*, London: Routledge

Cummins, H. (2005) Mommy tracking single women in academia when they are not mommies. *Women's Studies International Forum*, 28 (2,3)

Davies, A. and Thomas, R. (2001) Managerialism and accountability in higher education: the gendered nature of restructuring and the costs to academic service. *Critical Perspectives on Accounting*, 13

Dearlove, J. (1997) The academic labour process: from collegiality and professionalism to managerialism and proletarianisation? *Higher Education Review*, 30 (1)

Deem, R. and Johnson, R. (2003) Risking the university? Learning to be a manager-academic in UK universities, *Sociological Research Online*, 8 (3) http://www.socresonline.org.uk/8/3/deem.html

Deem, R. (1998) 'New managerialism' and higher education: the management of performances and cultures in universities in the United Kingdom. *International Studies in Sociology of Education*, 8 (1)

Deem, R. (2003) Gender, organisational cultures and the practices of manager-academics in UK universities. *Gender, Work and Organisation*, 10 (2)

Delanty, G. (2001) *Challenging knowledge*, Buckingham: Open University Press

Dempsey, B. (2003) Letter. Earn the respect. *Times Higher Education Supplement*

Department of Health (1999) *NHS zero tolerance zone resource pack*. Available at http://www.nhs.uk/zerotolerance/downloads. Accessed 29th May 2005

DeSouza, E. (2003) Contrapower sexual harassment: a survey of students and faculty members. *Sex Roles*, 1

Dooris, M. (1999) The health promoting university as a framework for promoting positive mental well being. *International Journal of Mental Health Promotion*, 1 (4)

Dzeich, B.W. and Weiner, L. (1984) *The lecherous professor: sexual harassment on campus*, Boston: Beacon Press

Einarsen, S. (1999) The nature and causes of bullying at work. *International Journal of Manpower*, 20 (1 /2)

Epstein, D. (1997) Keeping them in their place: hetero/sexist harassment, gender and the enforcement of heterosexuality. In Thomas, A. and Kitzinger, C. (eds) *Sexual harassment*, Buckingham: Open University Press

Evans, G.R. and Gill, J. (2001) *Universities and Students*, London: Kogan Page

Eyre, L. (2001) The discursive framing of sexual harassment in a university community. *Gender and Education*, 12 (3)

Farley, L. (1978) *Sexual shakedown*, London: Melbourne House

Field, T. (1996) *Bully in sight*, Wantage: Success Unlimited

Fine, R. (1997) *Being stalked*, London: Chatto and Windus

Fitzgerald, L. F. and Weitzman, L.M. (1990) Men who harass: speculation and data. In Paludi, M.A. (ed) *Ivory power: sexual harassment on campus*, Albany: State University of New York

Fleming, P. and Harvey, H. (2002) Strategy development in dealing with violence against employees in the workplace. *The Journal of the Royal Society for the Promotion of Health*, 122 (4)

Fox, S. and Stallworth, L. (2005) Racial/ethnic bullying: exploring the links between bullying and racism in the US workplace. *Journal of Vocational Behaviour,* 66

Furedi, F. (2001) Under the hammer. *Times Higher Education Supplement,* February 9th

Gillespie, T. (1996) Rape crisis centres and male rape: a face of the backlash. In Hester, M. Kelly, L. and Radford, J. (eds) *Women, violence and male power,* Buckingham: Open University Press

Goodey, J. (1997) Boys don't cry: masculinities, fear of crime and fearlessness. *British Journal of Criminology,* 37 (3)

Grahame, K. (2004) Contesting diversity in the academy: resistance to women of colour teaching race, class and gender. *Race, Gender and Class,* 11 (3)

Grauerholz, E. (1996). Sexual harassment in the academy: the case of women professors. In Stockdale, M. (ed) *Sexual harassment in the workplace,* London: Sage

Gutek, B. and Morasch, B. (1982) Sex ratios, sex-role spillover, and sexual harassment of women at work, *Journal of Social Issues,* 38 (4)

Hadjifotiou, N. (1983) *Women and harassment at work,* London: Pluto

Hall, R. and Sandler, B. (1984) *The classroom climate: a chilly one for women?* Washington DC: Project on the Status of Women

Halson, J. (1991) Young women, sexual harassment and heterosexuality: violence, power relations and mixed-sex schooling. In Abbott, P. and Wallace, C. (eds) *Gender, power and sexuality,* London: Macmillan

Harlow, R. (2003) 'Race doesn't matter, but...': the effect of race on professors' experiences and emotion management in the undergraduate college classroom. *Social Psychology Quarterly,* 66 (4)

Haywood, C. and Mac an Ghaill, M. (2003) *Men and masculinities,* Buckingham: Open University Press

Health and Safety Executive (2004) *Violence at work. A guide for employers,* London: HSE. Available at www.hse.gov.uk. Accessed 17th June 2005

Hearn, J. and Parkin, W. (2001) *Gender, sexuality and violence in organizations,* London: Sage

Hellzen, O. Asplund, K. Sandman, P-O and Norberg, A. (2004) The meaning of caring as described by nurses caring for a person who acts provokingly: an interview study. *Scandinavian Journal of Caring Sciences,* 18

Henwood, K. and Procter, J. (2003) The 'good father': reading men's accounts of paternal involvement during the transition to first-time fatherhood. *British Journal of Social Psychology,* 42

Herbert, C. (1989) *Talking of silence: the sexual harassment of school girls,* London: Falmer

Hey, V. (2003) Joining the club? Academia and working-class femininities. *Gender and Education,* 15 (3)

Hinze, S. (2004) 'Am I being over-sensitive?': women's experience of sexual harassment during medical training. *Health: an interdisciplinary journal for the social study of health, illness and medicine,* 8 (1)

Hoel, H. and Cooper, C. (2000) *Destructive conflict and bullying at work,* Manchester: UMIST

Hughes, C. (2002) Pedagogies of, and for, resistance. In Howie, G. and Tauchert, A. (eds) *Gender, teaching and research in higher education: challenges for the 21st century*, Aldershot: Ashgate

Iantaffi, A. (1996) Women and disability in higher education: a literature search. In Morley, L. and Walsh, V. (eds) *Breaking boundaries: women in higher education*, London: Taylor and Francis

Ishmael, A. (1999) *Harassment, bullying and violence at work*, London: Industrial Society

Jackson, D., Clare, J. and Mannix, J. (2002) Who would want to be a nurse? Violence in the workplace – a factor in recruitment and retention. *Journal of Nursing Management*, 10

Jackson, S. (2000) Differently academic? Constructions of 'academic' in higher education. *Higher Education Research and Development*, 19 (3)

Jackson, S. (2002) Transcending boundaries: women, research and teaching in the academy. In: Howie, G. and Tauchert, A. (eds) *Gender, teaching and research in higher education: challenges for the 21st century*, Aldershot: Ashgate

Johnson, R. (2002) Learning to manage the university: tales of training and experience. *Higher Education Quarterly*, 56 (1)

Johnson, R. and Deem, R. (2003) Talking of students: tensions and contradictions in the manager-academic and the university in contemporary higher education. *Higher Education*, 46

Jones, C. (1985) Sexual tyranny: male violence in a mixed secondary school. In Weiner, G. (ed) *Just a bunch of girls*, Buckingham: Open University Press

Kelly, L. (1988) *Surviving sexual violence*, Cambridge: Polity

Kerfoot, D. and Whitehead, S. (2000) Keeping all the balls in the air: further education and the masculine/managerial subject. *Journal of Further and Higher Education*, 24 (2)

King, T. (1995) Witness us in our battles: four student projections of Black female academics. *Journal of Organizational Change Management*, 8 (6)

Kinman, G. and Jones, F. (2003) Running up the down escalator: stressors and strains in UK academics. *Quality in Higher Education*, 9 (1)

Kitzinger, C. (1994) Anti-lesbian harassment. In Brant, C. and Too, Y.L. (eds) *Rethinking sexual harassment*, London: Pluto

Knights, D. and Richards, W. (2003) Sex discrimination in UK academia, *Gender, Work and Organisation*, 10 (2)

Körner, B. (2002) Feminist pedagogy and personal engagement in higher education. In Howie, G. and Tauchert, A. (eds) *Gender, teaching and research in higher education*, Aldershot: Ashgate

Kosson, D.S., Kelly, J.C. and White, J.W (1997) Psychopathy-related traits predict self-reported sexual aggression among college men. *Journal of Interpersonal Violence*, 12 (2)

Kuhlenschmidt, S. and Layne, L. (1999) Strategies for dealing with difficult behaviour. *New Directions for Teaching and Learning*, 77

Lahelma, E., Palmu, T. and Gordon, T. (2000) Intersecting power relations in teachers' experiences of being sexualised or harassed by students. *Sexualities*, 3

Leathwood, C. (2000) Happy families? Pedagogy, management and parental discourses of control in the corporative further education college. *Journal of Further and Higher Education*, 24 (2)

Lee, D. (1998) Sexual harassment in PhD supervision. *Gender and Education*, 10 (3)

Lee, D. (2000a) An analysis of workplace bullying in the UK. *Personnel Review*, 29 (5)

Lee, D. (2000b) Hegemonic masculinity and male feminisation: the sexual harassment of men at work. *Journal of Gender Studies* 9 (2)

Lee, D. (2001) 'He didn't sexually harass me, as in harassed for sex ... he was just horrible': women's definitions of unwanted male sexual conduct at work, *Women's Studies International Forum*, 24 (1)

Lee, D. (2002a) Gendered workplace bullying in the restructured UK Civil Service. *Personnel Review*, 31 (2)

Lee, D (2002b) Interpersonal abuse on campus. Paper presented at the Interpersonal Abuse: Multi-agency and interdisciplinary approaches conference, University of Derby, June 2002

Lee, D. (2003) Give me an A or you're dead. *Times Higher Education Supplement*, February 28th

Lee, D. (2004) An exploratory analysis of the gender dynamics of unacceptable student conduct. Paper presented at the Women in Higher Education Conference, Bolton Institute, May 2004

Lee, D. (2005a) Women's experiences of unacceptable student conduct and subsequent managerial intervention. Paper presented at the Fifth International Gender and Education Association Conference, Cardiff University, March 2005

Lee, D. (2005b) Students and managers behaving badly: an exploratory analysis of the vulnerability of feminist academics in anti-feminist, market-driven UK higher education. *Women's Studies International Forum*, 28 (2-3)

Lees, S. (1997) *Ruling passions*, Buckingham: Open University Press

Leonard, D. (2001) *A woman's guide to doctoral studies*, Buckingham: Open University Press

Lerum, K. (2004) Sexuality, power and camaraderie in service work. *Gender and Society*, 18 (6)

Letherby, G. (2002) Claims and disclaimers: knowledge, reflexivity and representation in feminist research. *Sociological Research Online*, 6 (4) http://www.socresonline.org.uk/6/4/letherby.html

Letherby, G. and Marchbank, J. (2001) Why do Women's Studies?: A cross-England profile. *Women's Studies International Forum*, 24 (5)

Letherby, G. and Sheils, J. (2001) 'Isn't he good, but can we take her seriously?': gendered expectations in higher education. In Anderson, P. and Williams, J. (eds) *Identity and difference in higher education*, Aldershot: Ashgate

Lewis, D. (2004) Bullying at work: the impact of shame among university and college lecturers. *British Journal of Guidance and Counselling*, 32 (3)

Leymann, H. (1990) Mobbing and psychological terror at workplaces. *Violence and Victims*, 5

Liddle, J. and Widdowson, B. (1997) Women, violence and the trade union. *Indian Journal of Gender Studies*, 4 (1)

Liefooghe, A. and Olafsson, R. (1999) 'Scientists' and 'amateurs': mapping the bullying domain. *International Journal of Manpower,* 20 (1 / 2)

Lipsett, A. (2005) Bullying rife across campus. *Times Higher Education Supplement,* September 16th

Lucero, M. Middleton, K. Finch, W. and Valentine, S. (2003) An empirical investigation of sexual harassers: toward a perpetrator typology. *Human Relations,* 56 (12)

Luke, C. (1994) Women in the academy: the politics of speech and silence. *British Journal of Sociology of Education,* 15 (2)

McKenna, B. Poole, S. Smith, N. Coverdale, J. and Gale, C. (2003) A survey of threats and violent behaviour by patients against registered nurses in their first year of practice. *International Journal of Mental Health Nursing,* 12

McKinney, K. and Crittenden, K. (1992) Contrapower sexual harassment: the offender's viewpoint. *Free Inquiry in Creative Sociology,* 20 (1)

Maguire, M. (1996) Older women in higher education. In Morley, L. and Walsh, V. (eds) *Breaking boundaries: women in higher education,* London: Taylor and Francis

Maguire, M. (2001) Beating time?: the resistance, reproduction and representation of older women in teacher education (UK). *International Journal of Inclusive Education,* 5 (2, 3)

Manufacturing, Science and Finance trade union [now Amicus] (1994) *Bullying at work: confronting the problem.* Report of a Conference organised by MSF, 24th May 1994. London: MSF

Marchbank, J. and Letherby, G. (2002) Offensive and defensive: student support and higher education evaluation. In Howie, G. and Tauchert, A. (eds) *Gender, teaching and research in higher education: challenges for the 21st century,* Aldershot: Ashgate

Matchen, J. and DeSouza, E. (2000) The sexual harassment of faculty members by students. *Sex Roles,* 42 (3, 4)

Mayhew, C. McCarthy, P. Barker, M. and Sheehan, M. (2003) Student aggression in tertiary education institutions. *Journal of Occupational Health and Safety, Australia and New Zealand,* 19 (4)

Messner, M. (2000) White guy habitus in the classroom. *Men and Masculinities,* 2 (4)

Mikkelsen, E. and Einarsen, S. (2002) Basic assumptions and symptoms of post-traumatic stress among victims of bullying at work. *European Journal of Work and Organisational Psychology,* 11 (1)

Monaghan, L. (2004) Doorwork and legal risk: observations from an embodied ethnography. *Social and Legal Studies,* 13 (4)

Moore, M. (1997) Student resistance to course content: reactions to the gender of the messenger. *Teaching Sociology,* 25

Morley, L. (1999) *Organising feminisms,* Basingstoke: Macmillan

Morley, L. (2002) Lifelong yearning: feminist pedagogy in the learning society. In Howie, G. and Tauchert, A. (eds) *Gender, teaching and research in higher education,* Aldershot: Ashgate

Morley, L. (2003) *Quality and power in higher education,* Buckingham: Open University Press

Munn, P. (1992) Ways of improving discipline in secondary schools and class-rooms. In Jones, N. and Baglin Jones, E. (eds) *Learning to behave*, London: Kogan Page

Munn-Giddings, C. (1998) Mixing motherhood and academia – a lethal cocktail. In Malina, D. and Maslin-Prothero, S. (eds) *Surviving the academy: feminist perspectives*, London: Falmer

Murrell, A. (1996) Sexual harassment and women of colour: issues, challenges and future directions. In Stockdale, M. (ed) *Sexual harassment in the workplace*, London: Sage

National Association for Teachers in Further and Higher Education [NATFHE] (2005) *Student complaints: NATFHE advice to higher education branches*. Published September 2005. Available at www.natfhe.org.uk. Accessed 13th October 2005

National Committee of Inquiry into Higher Education (1997) *Higher education in the learning society*. London: NCIHE

New, C. (2001) Oppressed and oppressors? The systematic mistreatment of men. *Sociology*, 35 (3)

Nicol, D. (2000) Preparation and support of part-time teachers in higher education. *Teacher Development*, 4 (1)

North, M. (2005) When the hugs don't work... *The Times Higher Education Supplement*, July 22nd 2005

O'Beirne, M., Denney, D., Gabe, J., Elston, M. and Lee, R. (2003) Veiling violence. In Lee, R. and Stanko, E. (eds) *Researching violence*, London: Routledge

O'Leary-Kelly, A.M. Paetzold, R.L. and Griffin, R.W. (2000) Sexual harassment as aggressive behaviour: an actor-based perspective. *Academy of Management Review*, 25 (2)

Osborne, R. (1995) The continuum of violence against women in Canadian universities. *Women's Studies International Forum*, 18 (5/6)

Osgood Smith, J., Whitman, J., Grant, P., Stanutz, A., Russett, J. and Rankin, K. (2001) Peer networking as a dynamic approach to supporting new faculty. *Innovative Higher Education*, 25 (3)

Palfreyman, D. and Warner, D. (1998) Setting the scene. In Palfreyman, D. and Warner, D. (eds) *Higher education and the law*, Buckingham: Open University Press

Patai, D. (1998) Galloping contradictions: sexual harassment in academe. *Gender Issues*, 16 (1, 2)

Paton, G. and Seth, M. (2005) Ill-prepared to cope with the 'classroom yobs'. *Times Educational Supplement*, 29th July

Pervin, K. and Turner, A. (1998) A study of bullying of teachers by pupils in an inner London school. *Pastoral Care*, 16 (4)

Probert, B. (2005) 'I just couldn't fit it in': gender and unequal outcomes in academic careers. *Gender, Work and Organisation*, 12 (1)

Quine, L. (2002) Workplace bullying in junior doctors: questionnaire survey. *British Medical Journal*, 324

Quinn, J. (2004) Mothers, learners and countermemory. *Gender and Education*, 16 (3)

Race, P. (1999) *How to get a good degree*, Buckingham: Open University Press

Race, P. (2001) How to increase students' motivation. *Educational Developments*, 1 (4)

Rapaport, K. and Burkhart, B.R. (1984) Personality and attitudinal characteristics of sexually coercive college males. *Journal of Abnormal Psychology*, 93

Rayner, C. (1997) Incidence of workplace bullying. *Journal of Community and Applied Social Psychology*, 7 (3)

Rayner, C. (1999) From research to implementation: finding leverage for prevention. *International Journal of Manpower*, 20 (1 / 2)

Rayner, C. Hoel, H. and Cooper, C. (2002) *Workplace bullying: what we know, who is to blame, and what can we do?* London: Taylor and Francis

Ritzer, G. (1996) McUniversity in the postmodern consumer society. *Quality in Higher Education*, 2 (3)

Robinson, K. (2000) 'Great tits, miss!'. The silencing of male students' sexual harassment of female teachers in secondary schools: a focus on gendered authority. *Discourse: studies in the cultural politics of education*, 21 (1)

Rogers, B. (2000) *Cracking the hard class: strategies for managing the harder than average class*, London: Sage

Roiphe, K. (1994) *The morning after*, London: Hamish Hamilton

Salin, D. (2003) Ways of explaining workplace bullying: a review of enabling, motivating and precipitating structures and processes in the work environment. *Human Relations*, 56 (10)

Samuels, H. (2003) Sexual harassment in the workplace: a feminist analysis of recent developments in the UK. *Women's Studies International Forum*, 26 (5)

Saunderson, W. (2002) Women, academia and identity: constructions of equal opportunities in the 'new managerialism' – a case of lipstick on the gorilla? *Higher Education Quarterly*, 56 (4)

Schneider, J., Weerakoon, P. and Heard, R. (1999) Inappropriate client sexual behaviour in occupational therapy. *Occupational Therapy International*, 6 (3)

Schneider, M. and Phillips, S. (1997) A qualitative study of sexual harassment of female doctors by patients. *Social Science and Medicine*, 45 (5)

Secker, J., Benson, A., Balfe, E., Lipsedge, M., Robinson, S. and Walker, J. (2004) Understanding the social context of violent and aggressive incidents on an inpatient unit. *Journal of Psychiatric and Mental Health Nursing*, 11

Sharpe, R. (2000) A framework for training graduate teaching assistants. *Teacher Development*, 4 (1)

Shaw, M. (2005) Big rise in attacks on staff. *Times Educational Supplement*, 29th July

Shevlin, M. Banyard, P. Davies, M. and Griffiths, M. (2000) The validity of student evaluation of teaching in higher education. *Assessment and Evaluation in Higher Education*, 25 (4)

Simpson, R. and Cohen, C. (2004) Dangerous work: the gendered nature of bullying in the context of higher education. *Gender, Work and Organization*, 11 (2)

Stanko, E. (1996) Reading danger: sexual harassment, anticipation and self proection. In Hester, M. Kelly, L. and Radford, J. (eds) *Women, violence and male power*, Buckingham: Open University Press

Stanko, E. and Hobdell, K. (1993) Assault on men. Masculinity and male victimization. *British Journal of Criminology*, 33 (3)

Stockdale, M. (1996) What we know and what we need to learn about sexual harassment. In Stockdale, M. (ed) *Sexual harassment in the workplace*, London: Sage

Terry, A. (1998) Teachers as targets of bullying by their pupils: a study to investigate incidence. *British Journal of Educational Psychology*, 68 (2)

Thomas, A. (1997) Men behaving badly? A psychosocial exploration of the cultural context of sexual harassment. In Thomas, A. and Kitzinger, C. (1997) (eds) *Sexual harassment*, Buckingham: Open University Press

Thomas, A. (2004) Politics, policies and practice: assessing the impact of sexual harassment policies in UK universities. *British Journal of Sociology of Education*, 25 (2)

Thompson, S. (1998) Who goes there, friend or foe? Black women, white women and friendships in academia. In Malina, D. and Maslin-Prothero, S. (eds) *Surviving the academy: feminist perspectives*, London: Falmer

Titus, J. (2000) Engaging student resistance to feminism: 'how is this stuff going to make us better teachers?' *Gender and Education*, 12

Troman, G. (2003) Coping collectively: the formation of a teacher self-help group. *British Journal of Sociology of Education*, 24 (2)

Tutor A and Tutor B (1996) *Trix of the grade*, Aldershot: Gower

Union of Shop, Distributive and Allied Workers (2002) Press release. Abuse is not part of the job. USDAW. Available at http://www.usdaw.org.uk. Accessed 17th June 2005

Upson, A. (2004) *Violence at work: findings from the 2002/2003 British Crime Survey*, London: Home Office

Verkuyten, M. (2002) Making teachers accountable for students' disruptive classroom behaviour. *British Journal of Sociology of Education*, 23 (1)

Viitasara, E. and Menckel, E. (2002) Developing a framework for identifying individual and organizational risk factors for the prevention of violence in the health-care sector. *Work*, 19

Waddington, P.A.J., Badger, D. and Bull, R. (2005) Appraising the inclusive definition of workplace 'violence'. *British Journal of Criminology*, 45

Walsh, V. (2005) Gender, narrative, (mental) health: the missing conversation. Unpublished paper

Walton, C., Coyle, A. and Lyons, E. (2004) Death and football: an analysis of men's talk about emotions. *British Journal of Social Psychology*, 43

Webber, M. (2005) 'Don't be so feminist': exploring student resistance to feminist approaches in a Canadian university. *Women's Studies International Forum*, 28 (2-3)

Wheeler, S. and Birtle, J. (1993) *A handbook for personal tutors*, Buckingham: Open University Press

Whitbread, A. (1989) Female teachers are women first: sexual harassment at work. In Spender, D. and Sarah, E. (eds) *Learning to lose*, London: Women's Press

Whitehead, A. (2003) The legacy of a violent attack: an exploratory study of occupational therapy students' experiences of violent attack. *British Journal of Occupational Therapy*, 66 (3)

Wilson, F. (2000) The social construction of sexual harassment and assault of university students. *Journal of Gender Studies*, 9 (2)

Wilson, F. (2005) Caught between difference and similarity: the case of women academics. *Women in Management Review*, 20 (4)

Wise, S. and Stanley, L. (1987) *Georgie porgie*, London: Pandora

Wragg, E. Haynes, G. Wragg, C. and Chamberlin, R. (2000) *Failing teachers*, London: Routledge

www.oia.ac.uk. Accessed 11th November 2005

www.teachersupport.info. Accessed 11th November 2005

www.tqi.ac.uk. Accessed 11th November 2005

Zalk, S. R. (1990) Men in the academy: a psychological profile of harassment. In Paludi, M. (ed) *Ivory power: sexual harassment on campus*, Albany: State University of New York

Zapf, D. (1999) Organisational, work group related and personal causes of mobbing/bullying at work. *International Journal of Manpower*, 20 (1 / 2)

Index